Praise for *The Spirituality of Grief*

"*The Spirituality of Grief* is a pragmatic, intelligent, and heartfelt guide that will benefit anyone wandering through the journey of loss."

—**Rabbi Steve Leder,** *New York Times*–bestselling author of *The Beauty of What Remains* and *For You When I Am Gone*

"In *The Spirituality of Grief,* Fran Tilton Shelton uses personal experience, the stories of others, and in-depth research to give the griever a detailed yet user-friendly way to understand their grief in all its variations. In addition to providing compassionate understanding, she offers effective spiritual practices to bring peace into turmoil, light into darkness, and calm into the storm."

—**Jan Warner,** author of *Grief Day by Day*

"*The Spirituality of Grief* is the grief resource I didn't know I was longing for. In these pages, I found what felt like a conversation with a wise and trusted friend witnessing our grief and then inviting us into a more expansive and inclusive spirituality that both supports and heals. This book is an offering of love, experience, and practical tools. I can't wait to incorporate this valuable text into my grief classes and support groups, in addition to my own personal devotions."

—**Zeena Regis,** faith outreach and engagement manager, Compassion & Choices

"*The Spirituality of Grief* is a balm of comfort, written by someone who is well acquainted with the beautiful burden of grief and well equipped to walk as a companion with anyone on the long journey of sorrow. In reading this book, I had the profound sense of both seeing and being seen."

—**Amanda Held Opelt,** songwriter and author of *A Hole in the World*

T0049968

"Carrying the sorrow of a loved one's death will not end by reading this soon-to-be classic, but you will learn to carry grief differently. Fran Tilton Shelton equips us to lift our grief in ways that prevent us from falling under its weight. Combining the latest in academic research with case studies, spiritual exercises, and personal narrative, Shelton focuses on bereavement and the spirituality that can sustain us. She is a tender guide into a love stronger than death and into a way that we can love—even in separation."

—**Dr. Jeanne Stevenson-Moessner**, professor of
pastoral care and pastoral theology at
Perkins School of Theology

"If you are looking for someone who puts heartbreaking loss into conversation with the practices of faith—if you are looking for a companion who will walk alongside you with grace, humor, and hope—your search is over. This book is a gift."

—**Dr. Scott Black Johnston,** pastor of
Fifth Avenue Presbyterian Church

A beautiful book that is both practical and personal, sure to be a welcome guide for those who find themselves lost and awash in grief."

—**Rev. Nathan Carlin, PhD**, director of the
McGovern Center for Humanities and Ethics

The

Spirituality

of Grief

The
TEN PRACTICES FOR
Spirituality
THOSE WHO REMAIN
of Grief

FRAN TILTON SHELTON

Broadleaf Books

Minneapolis

THE SPIRITUALITY OF GRIEF
Ten Practices for Those Who Remain

What Am I Gonna Do (With The Rest Of My Life)
Words and Music by Merle Haggard

Copyright © 1983 Sony Songs LLC
All Rights Administered by Sony Music Publishing (US) LLC, 424 Church Street, Suite 1200, Nashville, TN 37219
International Copyright Secured All Rights Reserved
Reprinted by Permission of Hal Leonard LLC

"Litany of Release," written by Reverend Fran Pratt, is used by permission of the author. Find more of her resources at www.franpratt.com.

The poem "I Wish," written by Rabbi Zell, is used by permission of the author.

Excerpts from the writings of Elaine Gantz-Wright, Todd Atkins, and Nancy LeCroy in chapter 9 are used by permission of the authors.

Scripture quotations are taken from the New Revised Standard Version Updated Edition. Copyright © 2021 National Council of Churches of Christ in the United States of America. Used by permission. All rights reserved worldwide.

Interior illustrations by Asa Cole.

Cover image: Wave pattern: SEPARISA/AdobeStock
Cover design: Cindy Laun

Print ISBN: 978-1-5064-8310-8
eBook ISBN: 978-1-5064-8311-5

CONTENTS

CONTENTS

CHAPTER 1

HOW DO WE BEGIN? TELLING YOUR GRIEF STORY

Nothing can make up for the absence of someone we love, and it would be wrong to try to find a kind of substitute. We must simply hold out and see it through. This sounds very hard at first, but at the same time it is a great consolation, for the gap, as long as it remains unfilled, preserves the bonds between us. It is nonsense to say that God fills the gap. God doesn't fill it, but on the contrary God keeps it empty and so helps us keep alive our communion with each other even at the cost of pain.

—Dietrich Bonhoeffer

Grace and peace. These are the first words I say at the beginning of the bereavement workshops I lead. I speak the words slowly as I make eye contact with each participant. I gently repeat them: *grace and peace, grace and peace.* I pray that the words will permeate the deafening silence of fears, the syncopated sadness, and the questions that crowd the large room.

I pray that grace and peace will come to me, too. Through my work with Faith & Grief, a nonprofit I cofounded that provides resources for comfort to those who have experienced the death of a loved one, I have led many sessions like this. Yet no matter how many grief workshops I've facilitated, I always get anxious before the first meeting. I wonder who in the participants' families or networks have died and how their deaths occurred. I worry about how the group will gel, and I wonder if the participants are ready to accept invitations to share with the group.

Each participant has already demonstrated courage. Twice. First, in registering for the workshop. Second, in showing up for the beginning class. For people in the throes of raw, profound grief, these two acts can require tremendous effort.

You are demonstrating courage, too, by opening this book. When a loved one dies, what used to be simple decisions—return a phone call or not, make the bed or not, read this book or not—become difficult or almost impossible. And choosing to read a book that takes you deeper into the subject of grief rather than escape it takes courage.

In workshops, I promise that participants will be invited, not required, to share personal information over the course of our time together. The only requirements are that they attend all sessions, hold conversations in confidence, refrain from comparing their grief to that of others, and feel free to interrupt me at any point for clarification or to share an "aha moment." As you read this book, you too can engage to the extent that you desire. The ideas and practices these pages contain aren't requirements; they're invitations.

Then I invite workshop participants to silently read this quotation, attributed to Isak Dinesen: *All sorrows can be borne if we put them in a story or tell a story about them.*

A man of about seventy, attempting to hold steady a venti Starbucks on his knee, which is bouncing to the rhythm of an accelerated heartbeat, breaks the silence. "Isn't she the one who wrote *Out of Africa?*"

Yes, she is, I say. She also wrote *Babette's Feast*. His question is none other than grace verbalized, as it makes others feel more comfortable speaking. I ask, "How many of you have seen one or both of these movies?"

Some heads nod affirmatively while others murmur that they had heard of them. A young woman shares that she saw *Babette's Feast* in a college class. I tell the group that Isak Dinesen, the pen name for writer Karen Blixen, was nine years old when her father, riddled with syphilis and depressed after fathering two children out of wedlock, hanged himself. His death by suicide changed her life. The love Blixen held for her father never left, and she continued to yearn for his company and affection the rest of her life. But she also learned that in order to carry the weight of this sorrow and future sorrows, she needed to put her experiences, feelings, and questions in the form of a story.

"Just as Dinesen shared her story, we are going to begin to do the same," I tell the group. "Let's start by saying our first name, the name and relationship of our loved one who died, and when he, she, or they died. I'll begin. My name is Fran. Bob, my husband, died on March 4, 2018."

A few in the group begin to share, and some are unable to finish as emotion overcomes them. It is a difficult step to give voice to such love, to such pain, to such reality. For some, the most difficult part is saying the name of their loved one. Such a simple expression becomes a complicated task.

One woman admits that it feels good to say Brenden, her son's name, because it assures her that he is not forgotten. It bothers her that her friends won't say his name because they are afraid it will upset her. "They don't understand," she says, wiping away tears. "How can I be *more* upset? I'm always thinking of him."

Names are important. They give us our identity. Nicknames or pet names are equally meaningful, as they anchor us in our relationships and even in the timelines of our lives. When a person asks me about my husband by calling him *Gunner, Brownie, Robert, Dean Shelton, President Shelton,* or *BobBob,* I can put Bob in a certain place, time, or role.

Think about all the names friends and relatives called your loved one. How do those names reflect different parts his, her, or their life and story? And how might saying your loved one's name help you, over time, learn to carry your sorrow?

I wrote this book to guide you in learning to tell your story of love and grief. I hope that it can be a companion during a time that can be so shattering and terrifying and lonely and gut-wrenching that you wonder if you can even take another breath. Sharing our grief stories is a way of riding the waves of grief that wash over us after a loved one dies. Those waves can be so immense and powerful that in the middle of them, we may feel like we're going to be forever caught in the undertow. Yet with practice, we can begin to discern the pattern inherent in the waves: the approach, the rise, the crest, the break, and, finally, the way it settles. We can begin to trust that, eventually, the wave of grief will set us down on the shore.

This book is not designed to help you "move on" or "let go" or "find closure." Rather, it will help to sustain you and your connection with your loved one. It will expand your heart to trust that steady, solid ground is still there, beneath the tidal waves of grief. It will help you find your footing. And it will help you carry the weight of your grief.

HOW CAN WE CARRY OUR SORROW?

To some people, especially those experiencing raw grief, the concept of learning to carry our sorrow is a new and even unbearable one. When Isak Dinesen says, "All sorrows can be borne," we may wonder if she is telling the truth. The word *borne* comes from a Hebrew word meaning "to lift up" or "to carry." If your loved one has just died, the idea of carrying your sorrow sounds impossible. Just carrying the trash out to the curb may take all your strength these days. How can you begin to carry the weight of this immense, immovable grief?

When we bear our sorrows, though, we not only carry the sadness of our loved one's death but also all the stories of their life. By telling our grief stories, we discover an inner strength that equips us to lift, or carry, our sorrows rather than to be pulled down by them.

Many people experience a visceral desire to get over, walk around, or ignore their sorrow rather than carry it. Ron's wife died five months before he attended one of our workshops on faith and grief. He was disappointed that his daughter, their only child, wouldn't talk to him about her grief. But at the registration table for the workshop, he articulated something akin to his daughter's unwillingness to talk. "I just want to get over this and move on," he said.

I just want to get over this and move on: many people facing grief feel like Ron and his daughter. Even though he wanted to talk about their shared grief and she didn't, they both just wanted to "get over this and move on." Such desires spring from our self-preservation and survival instincts. We don't want to hurt more than we already do. Truth be told, however, it's impossible to hurt more than we already do.

Spirituality and faith offer important ways to carry our sorrow. When we open our hearts to the wisdom given to us from spiritual and religious traditions throughout history, we learn that bearing our sorrows will take us on paths we may not have traveled before. As we walk these paths, we slowly encounter insights into the mystery of love that is stronger than death, patience, compassion, solidarity, humility, and gratitude.

In the work of Faith & Grief, we see faith as a source of comfort and strength in times of bereavement. All faith traditions value grief and mourning and offer practices to sustain and give solace. We find that grief is both a leveler and a uniter, bringing together persons from diverse faith traditions and backgrounds. While I write as a Christian, you will see different faith traditions reflected in this book. Grief workshops bring together people from different faiths to share their stories and experience community. Time and again, we hear how spiritual practices give comfort and hope to those who remain.

Psalm 23 in the Hebrew scripture assures us, "Even though I walk through the darkest valley, I fear no evil; for you are with me; your rod and your staff—they comfort me." The psalmist does not avoid walking through the darkest valley because of an abiding trust that God will walk alongside him. Walking *through* the valley is both a description of grief and a prescription for working through it—step by step. Even as adults, we may feel intimidated or still have childlike fears of the darkness. We can't see where to step; we are anxious that some unseen object will trip us along the way or that we will get stuck in a miry bog.

Keep in mind that there is no prescribed time frame for grief. There is no shortcut, no spiritual bypass. The canyon or valley that forms inside us when our loved one dies will never go away. The sorrow that has taken up residence within us since the death of our loved one will never dissipate. Rather, through God's grace and mercy, we learn to forever carry our love for them and their love for us.

In this book, we will discover meaningful and spiritual ways to "keep alive our communion," as Dietrich Bonhoeffer wrote. Each chapter will focus on a central question that grief brings to us and a spiritual practice that can help us carry our sorrow. You can try these spiritual practices no matter what your faith or religious tradition might be. I offer these practices not to help you "get over" your grief or to "move on" or even to "heal." They are not intended to replace your grief with some substitute. As Bonhoeffer said: "Nothing can make up for the absence of someone we love." Instead, you could think of them as containers for your sorrow—something to put your sorrow in, to help you carry it.

WHY DO WE TELL OUR GRIEF STORIES?

Psychologists, brain scientists, and researchers have learned that a bond of hope is created between us when we engage in telling and listening to stories. Listening to and reading stories encourages the release of the hormones oxytocin and cortisol. Oxytocin controls responses such as empathy and social interaction. Cortisol is connected to reducing stress.

The release of these hormones better equips us to face the future, full of unknown circumstances, without the physical and emotional support of our deceased loved ones. Years ago, I overheard a workshop participant say, "Telling my story and having my feelings validated takes away much of the fear of grief." Similarly, a woman whose mother died from a glioblastoma said, "I feel stronger just by listening to what others have gone through. They help me believe I can cope, too."

Allan Hugh Cole Jr., theologian, professor, and author of *Good Mourning: Getting Through Your Grief*, stresses the importance of telling, retelling, or rehearsing one's story. He provides an image of the healing power of story. The word *hearse*, he tells us—a vehicle used to carry the dead body of a person in a coffin or casket to a funeral and cemetery—comes from the Latin word *hirpex,* which means "harrow."

A harrow is a trusty, rake-like toothed tool. Gardeners value the harrow because it helps them till and break up the soil for planting new growth in their flower and vegetable beds. Cole likens the telling of our personal sorrow to the work of a harrow. Each time we tell—or re*hearse*—our story, we are figuratively tilling the very soil of our soul, breaking up the crusty clay of emotions lodged in our heart so that new growth can take place.

Without being fully aware that we are doing so, we tend to rehearse certain parts of our stories. We tell and retell the parts that we are working to reconcile with the parts of our larger story. It is important to find people—such as a friend, counselor, bereavement group leader, spiritual director, or rabbi, priest, pastor, or imam—who understand the importance of rehearsing your story.

Back in the workshop on grief, as I describe the importance of telling our stories, one woman quickly speaks up. "I don't want a new life!" she tells the group. "I want my old life back with my husband. And I'm going to scream if one more person tells me that I must get used to a 'new normal.'" She makes air quotes with her fingers. "In fact, I might even punch them in the face."

Everyone laughs, and some raise their fists in solidarity. Sometimes people are surprised by the amount of laughter that takes place in a circle of storytelling. Experiencing these moments makes me more appreciative of the work of oxytocin and cortisol. Laughter can set us free to release immeasurable sadness and restock our bodies with endorphins.

The desire to have our life back "the way it was" is real. The desire of our friends to help us achieve a "new normal" is real as well. Even though these desires cannot be fulfilled, we long for them. And with each telling of our story, measures of healing *do* take place. In rehearsing our story, the rocky soil of resentment can be turned over for seeds of new growth. The alluvial soil flooded with tears of sadness can receive necessary air and light; the caliche, or hard sedimentary layer, can be broken and tenderized to keep it from becoming calcified.

Yet rehearsing our stories isn't some magic pill. Each telling takes courage and trust. Each telling may vary in the details, according to which portions of the story we need to process. The more opportunities to tell and rehearse our story, the greater the amount of healing. The more we can tell our stories, the greater our ease in carrying our love.

Because healing requires multiple tellings of our story, friends, family members, and colleagues sometimes grow weary of our repetitions. They may even say something bold or insensitive like, "You've told me that before," or "Again?" or "When are you going to get over this?"

Your friends mean well; they just don't get it! Keep telling your story. Again, if need be, find a professional to help you process your grief. You, and your grief story, are worth it.

When my husband was diagnosed with vascular dementia and Alzheimer's, he requested that I not tell anyone, including his adult children. I quickly made an appointment with Mary, a professional counselor. Mary is legally blind, which I believe heightens her ability to hear the stories her clients tell. She could not see my tsunami of tears, but she heard them with compassion week after week after week.

Mary listened to me tell of my anger toward Bob's neurologist when she informed us of his diagnosis and suggested that he exercise more. (Bob walked three miles a day and, in inclement weather, on the treadmill for an hour.) More? She listened when I told her about the fear that froze my blood when Bob got lost one day. She listened when I told her how much it meant to me when a nice salesman taught me how to tie a man's tie so I could dress Bob for his sister's funeral. She listened when I shared how, the day after Bob's own memorial service, I broke a tooth that led to months of dental work and literally could not smile for nine months after Bob's death. Mary listened as my tears surfaced and resurfaced, as I rehearsed my grief and love.

You are not alone on this journey. The spiritual practices in this book and the connections with others who have lost loved ones can help you ride the waves of grief.

LEARNING TO BREATHE

After a loved one dies, many people say they feel like their breath has been knocked out of them. After my grandmother's son, my uncle, died unexpectedly, she said,

"Since Rudy's death, I have not been able to take a deep breath."

Traditional Chinese medicine has a holistic view of the mind and the body. This tradition recognizes that grief and sadness directly affect the lungs. When individuals are unable to express emotions or are being overwhelmed by them, their lungs weaken, compromising respiration. Typically, this manifests as difficulty taking full breaths or the feeling that something is sitting on your chest. Some people have a flare-up of asthma, allergies, or bronchitis during times of sorrow. Perhaps some of these symptoms ring true for you. Just breathing through grief is harder than people think.

"When the breath is unsteady, all is unsteady. When the breath is still; all is still": this is wisdom commonly attributed to a sage named Goraksha, who lived in India in the ninth or tenth century. "Control the breath carefully. Inhalation gives strength and a controlled body; retention gives steadiness of mind and longevity; exhalation purifies body and spirit."

In seminary I was equally fascinated by the rough-and-tumble Hebrew language and the preciseness of Greek. My fascination grew as I learned that both the Hebrew word *ruach* and the Greek word *pneuma* (as in pneumatic) can be translated as "spirit" or "breath."

A spiritual practice of breath prayer can help you harrow the soil, aerating the ground of your griefs. In times when you're not sure you can cope, breathe. A breath prayer can help you transition from a state of anxiety to a place of peace.

Breath prayer has been around at least since the nineteenth century, most notably in *The Way of a Pilgrim*, first printed in 1891. This is a story about an unnamed Russian peasant who was curious about the Apostle Paul's imperative to the early church to "pray without ceasing" (1 Thessalonians 5:17). The wanderer traveled from place to place, seeking advice from scholars, priests, and sages about how to pray without ceasing. At last, a wise man unlocked the mystery for the pilgrim. "Breathe," the wise man said. Breathing is the one thing we do without thought and (most of the time) without pain.

The pilgrim began to think, pay attention, and notice the rhythm of his breathing. He began a pattern of prayer famously known as "The Jesus Prayer." With each inhale, he silently prayed, "Jesus Christ, Son of God," and he exhaled, praying, "have mercy on me, a sinner." He continued his travels while breathing this prayer.

Many faith traditions contain short prayers that can be used as breath prayers. As you learn and practice breath prayer, you might find that it helps you carry the weight of your grief.

SPIRITUAL PRACTICE

BREATH PRAYER

Breath prayer begins by visualizing and feeling God's heartwarming love and breath enter your body and expand your lungs. Through breath, God graciously gives you the essential thing you need to exist.

- Begin by noticing your breath. There is no need to change its pattern. Simply notice.

- Allow each exhale to release tension held in your body—beginning with your forehead, cheeks, and shoulders and moving all the way to your toes.

- When you are relaxed, inhale through your nose to the count of four, retain your breath to the count of four, and then exhale through your mouth to the count of four.

- Now add prayer. You can use a short prayer from your religious tradition. Or try this one.

> **Inhale,** *silently praying:* ***Creator of life and love,***
> **Hold:** *[visualize those you love]*
> **Exhale,** *silently praying:* ***Comfort me and strengthen me.***

- When your mind wanders (because that is what your mind is designed to do!), simply reengage in prayer with your next inhale.

- Write about your experience with a breath prayer. What feelings did you encounter? What thoughts ran through your mind?

CHAPTER 2

WHAT IS GRIEF? DEFINING THE TERMS

Grief is a tidal wave that overtakes you, smashes down upon you with unimaginable force, sweeps you up into its darkness, where you tumble and crash against unidentifiable surfaces, only to be thrown out on an unknown beach, bruised, reshaped. . . . It is the ashes from which the phoenix rises, and the mettle of rebirth. It returns life to the living dead. It teaches that there is nothing absolutely true or untrue. . . . Grief will make a new person out of you, if it doesn't kill you in the making.

—Stephanie Ericsson

In the first bereavement workshops that we offered through Faith & Grief, we would launch right into the dynamics and emotions of grief. Thankfully, at one workshop, a gentleman waved his arms in the air to stop us. "Whoa, whoa, wait a minute. Just what the hell is *bereavement*? What's *grief*? What's going on with me? I want you to start there." Others agreed with him.

Spending time defining terms like *bereavement* serves several purposes. It empowers us by putting words to the swirling contents of our hearts and minds. It also assists us in dismissing the off-putting comments from well-meaning sympathizers and the immeasurable number of euphemisms that offer plastic comfort. Many of us have heard things like, "So sorry to hear your mom passed," or "I'm glad she's in a better place," or "At least he's no longer in pain." Most euphemisms are well-intentioned. All of them miss the truth.

A young woman whose father had recently died said in one workshop, "So many people have told me they are 'sorry for my loss.'" She paused and looked around the room with wide eyes. "Um, my father is not *lost*. Trust me: if he was, I'd be looking for him. He's *dead*!"

Many people nodded in agreement. "When people say such a thing, it leaves such a bad taste in my mouth," she continued. "It's like when you take that last sip of orange juice after brushing your teeth."

Loss, bereavement, sorrow, mourning: we try to put so many words around the experience of grief. To that young woman, *loss* seemed to diminish or minimize rather than speak the truth about her father's death. While it's difficult to put words around the immensity of what we experience when a loved one dies, we can inch closer to understanding each other and others when we use words carefully. ·

One of my professors in seminary taught me an invaluable lesson: always define your terms. I can still hear his winsome yet commanding Scottish brogue instructing the class. "Write your own definition of terms," he insisted.

"Do not, under any circumstances, use *Merriam-Webster!*" Every writer owes their audience a definition of terms. This practice, my professor explained, demonstrates that the writer both knows the subject and acknowledges that there are other interpretations.

Providing definitions is especially important when writers are dealing with nuanced, personal topics like bereavement. Since our personal experiences are shaped by culture and faith, I'm going to share seven key definitions to lay some common ground. My definitions of grief, anticipatory grief, complicated grief, bereavement, disenfranchised grief, loss, and mourning come from my personal experiences, study, and a bit of creativity. I'm taking the liberty to paint some word pictures to help you grasp these key terms.

You may want to write your own definitions for these terms. Defining terms can be a cathartic process, and writing them down can guide you in figuring out what you know to be true about the words we use. Don't worry about getting your definitions exact or perfect, because no exact or perfect definitions exist. As Stephanie Ericsson says, and as you already know all too well: grief is a tidal wave. It's powerful, terrifying, shape-shifting. We'll look at this image of grief as a wave more later. For now, just remember that learning to ride the waves of grief is more important than getting the wording about it just right.

GRIEF

Grief comes from the French word *greve*, or "burden." Grief is an all-consuming, involuntary response—

emotional, physical, social, and spiritual—to detachment from someone or something that gives a person meaning, such as an end of relationship, vocation, or location. It is a burden on our very being.

Grief includes our response to the death of a loved one. It also refers to our feelings in the wake of many other kinds of life-changing events. My grief experiences are diverse, and yours likely are as well. At five years of age, I stood by my grandmother and watched her cry. We were looking through a second-story window at her lush backyard, where potential buyers were discussing a possible contract to purchase their home—a contract that would restore financial solvency to my grandparents. Another time, I watched my dad walk through the front door after being jailed for driving while intoxicated. One morning, I awoke to the news that my best friend and her mom had died in a car crash. There was the day a doctor told me that my dad hadn't made it through surgery and the one when I had to declare both personal and corporate bankruptcy. I failed my first oral examination for ordination. I watched my larger-than-life grandmother dwindle and die. And I sat dumbstruck as I learned that my husband had been diagnosed with vascular dementia and Alzheimer's. All these situations evoked grief.

In many grief workshops, participants are encouraged to take an inventory of the variety of griefs they have experienced. Take some time to reflect on times that you've walked through valleys of grief. Maybe it was a loss of job, a divorce, a natural disaster, a physical injury, the failure of a dream, or a medical diagnosis. What inner strength, change of heart, or wisdom did you acquire in the valley? How did you cope?

A grief inventory provides awareness that you have, by grace, managed to work through past traumatic events and that you are still standing. With reflection, you may recognize that not only are you still standing (maybe even a little taller); you've also cultivated greater compassion for others and a wisdom unattainable without sorrow.

While the sorrow that has surfaced in your mind about a past event is likely not nearly of the same magnitude as the death of your loved one—unless it was also a death—it is nonetheless a part of your history. These past experiences of grief are stepping-stones in this present valley of sorrow.

ANTICIPATORY GRIEF

Anticipatory grief is similar to grief except it occurs *before* the end of a relationship, employment, or geographical move. Persons also experience anticipatory grief while waiting for amputation of a limb or an organ transplant. Anticipatory grief carries similar emotional and behavioral responses as grief; however, emotions such as sadness, fear, and hope are usually heightened. A friend who was waiting for a lung transplant was overcome with sadness knowing that death would come to a person, and the person's family, for her to live. Fear expands as we attempt to imagine what the future will look like.

Anticipatory grief could also be known as *anxiety grief.* Anxiety is always future-oriented and involves imagining future possibilities. Recently a woman shared that *before* her husband was diagnosed with a terminal disease, they easily talked about what they would do in any number of future hypothetical scenarios. *After* his diagnosis, however, they could not bring themselves to talk openly about their circumstance. She was full of anxiety. These imaginings and anxieties come in the form of questions that are shaped by the circumstances.

After a medical diagnosis: What if the treatment doesn't work, or I don't get into the trial? Will I ever feel healthy again? Can I keep my job? What happens if I become disabled? How on earth will I pay these medical bills?

As a category, anticipatory grief has come to the forefront due to medical and pharmaceutical advances that have changed some terminal diagnoses into manageable diseases, but not yet curable illnesses. With these advances, individuals may enjoy more time with their families and friends before they die, but they are fully cognizant that death is coming. With that time comes an unspoken anticipatory grief question: "How long?"

Research is underway to further understand the heightened emotional responses associated with anticipatory grief. One Swedish study focused on caregivers who had family members in palliative care. The testing instrument, which still needs validation, revealed that 40 percent of female caregivers found that anticipatory grief was "more stressful" than the bereavement that occurred after their loved one died. I strongly identify with those women. Frankly, I am surprised it is not a higher percentage. When my husband didn't want to tell his children that he had been diagnosed with vascular dementia and Alzheimer's, my stress level soared. He remembered the trauma they had experienced thirty years prior when their mother had been diagnosed with cancer that later caused her death, and he wanted to protect them from the knowledge of his illness as long as he could.

Regrettably, anticipatory grief does not take the place of grief or a mourning process. Instead, it means that you will go through the grieving process twice. Knowing that the end of a relationship, job, or life that we've come to know is approaching at an unknown speed hinders our ability to function. The emotional energy it takes to hold hope and fear in tension compounds the stress of anticipatory grief. On one hand, we hope. On the other hand, we fear. Batting these emotions back and forth is like a wild game of ping pong. Attempting to ignore these feelings is as impossible as trying to hold an inflated beach ball underwater. They keep resurfacing.

So how can we mindfully manage hope and fear? I utilize two practices to mindfully manage my hope and fears: one is a Buddhist practice; the other, a practice rooted in my memories of an elementary school science experiment about the surface tension of water. These two practices may seem unexpected coming from a Presbyterian pastor with two grandsons in elementary school; however, they help me, and I hope they will you.

First, a practice emerging from Buddhism: as soon as Hope and Fear knock at the threshold of your heart, open the door wide. Welcome the visitors, and see that they make themselves comfortable. Offer them—and yourself—a cup of tea and shortbread. Once settled, begin a conversation with Hope and Fear through your imagination. Let your curiosity guide the conversation. Questions you might ask include the following: When have we met before? Where have you come from? What would you like to teach me? How long have you been traveling together? Listen carefully to what they have to say. Don't be shy about asking for clarification. Write their responses in a journal, if possible. In befriending Hope and Fear together, you may find new energy and insights.

Another way to visualize these emotions that are common in anticipatory grief is to think of them as elements in a science experiment. Visualize *hope* as cool, clear, calm water in a large glass bowl. Gaze at the water's beauty. Now visualize or begin placing ping-pong balls, each one representing a specific *fear*, on top of the water. Notice how the fears serenely float on the surface of hope. Imagining or seeing that the bowl of hope-filled water is much larger than all our fears may be enough to sustain you for the moment and days ahead.

While caring for Bob through our six-year journey with Alzheimer's, I made use of every visual image I could. I needed every single one that I could summon to find the nurturing skills, patience, joy, hope, and love during that time. If visual images are helpful to you, find one that speaks to you in your anticipatory grief and come back to it throughout the day.

COMPLICATED GRIEF

Complicated grief manifests in intense emotional and social relationships and lasts for more than a year. In some instances, the complication comes through what is known as *compound grief*. This occurs when multiple griefs occur within a short period of time, such as several deaths (persons or pets), diagnosis of a degenerative disease such as Alzheimer's or Parkinson's, and accidents that require lengthy rehabilitation.

Dr. Kimberly Shapiro, a psychiatrist and medical director, observes that about 10 percent of individuals experience complicated grief that inhibits their ability to function. Symptoms of complicated grief include "intense yearning for the loved one, preoccupation with memories involving the loved one, identity confusion, disbelief, avoidance of reminders of the death, intense emotional pain (including loneliness), difficulty engaging with others, emotional numbness, feelings that life is meaningless, and suicidal thoughts."

BEREAVEMENT

Bereavement is grief related to the death of a loved one. While this book could help people walk through a variety of types of grief, it focuses on bereavement and the spirituality that can sustain us when a loved one dies.

Bereavement is jam-packed with a dynamic entanglement of emotional, social, financial, physical, and spiritual upheavals. Individuals in bereavement have been deprived and made to feel desolate by the death of a loved one. Bereavement is at once the simplest grief to describe and one of the most difficult experiences to undergo.

Before the death of our loved one, we were attached—psychologically connected—to each other. Death detached us. John Bowlby, a nineteenth-century British psychologist best known for his influential work in attachment theory, understood attachment as a lasting psychological connection between human beings. This connectedness begins with an infant's innate need to form an attachment bond with a caregiver. This innate desire to attach helps us survive, regulate emotions, and develop relationships throughout life.

Bereavement is the emotional experience of detachment by death. The ramifications of this detachment, as Bowlby's work discovered, give us a visible understanding of our grief. We are painfully torn apart, or detached, from someone who has given us identity, pleasure, security, and meaning in life.

One of the primary philosophies of Hinduism, the third-largest religion in the world, is rooted in detachment. When doctoral student Ketika Garg's mother died, Ketika was grateful for her Hindu rituals. They helped her understand what is difficult to grasp: that the physical body perishes but the soul lives on. Following tradition, her mother was cremated. On the thirteenth day of mourning, the ceremony Preta-karma takes place to release the soul to support reincarnation. The loved one's ashes are then placed in an ocean or river, preferably the River Ganges. "The Song of God" from the Hindu text Bhagavad Gita gives assurance that the soul lives on:

> It is not born, it does not die;
> Having been, it will never be.

Unborn, eternal, constant and primordial;
It is not killed, when the body is killed.

Countless rituals of bereavement exist throughout the world as a result of different cultures and religions finding ways to metabolize grief. There are over 6.5 million Indigenous people in the world, and death rituals vary according to tribe. All such rituals are viewed to prepare the deceased for a spiritual journey. Many of the death rituals are tied to the tribe's traditional creation stories. Eugene Harry, a member of First Nation in British Columbia and a minister, reveres this connection. As a child, he learned that the Creator picked up a handful of beautiful red dirt, blew his breath on the dirt, and threw it into the sky. Starlight touched the red dirt and when the dust settled, the first man was standing on the earth. When a loved one dies, therefore, red powder is painted on the body in preparation for burial. The ritual begins with a line of paint placed below one eye and the deceased is told, "Look at the light, do not be afraid." Powder is placed on various places on the dead body. After this ritual, the body is washed, dressed, and buried.

Rituals help us visualize and verbalize sighs that are too deep for words. My grandmother recalled a funeral service for a young boy who had died in a car crash. At the church doors, before beginning the funeral procession, the Episcopal priest released a wail that reverberated within the stone-walled, stained-glass sanctuary. Silence absorbed the primordial sound waves. Then, and only then, did the priest speak Scripture: "The LORD is near to the brokenhearted and saves the crushed in spirit" (Psalm 34:18).

DISENFRANCHISED GRIEF

Disenfranchised grief is grief or bereavement that is ignored or rebuked by society and employers. Others' responses to our bereavement and grief are often, at best, awkward. Those on the receiving end initially hear these comments with politeness, to cover hurt feelings. For example, after my dad died, my mom was told, "You should feel lucky that Bill died quickly, because the cancer could have been long and drawn out." My mother did not feel lucky.

Disenfranchised grief doesn't receive even awkward responses. It exists when *no* response is extended or when a person's life-changing sorrow is casually brushed off. In these circumstances, a whirlpool of questions swirl within the survivor's heart. Is my pain real? Are my feelings normal? Should I be acting differently? What is the matter with me?

Stories of women or couples who experience a miscarriage and people who experience the death of a sibling who don't receive support suggest that disenfranchised grief is real. A surviving partner often experiences disenfranchised grief when a marriage has not taken place. The years and years that the two have lived together, in the home they purchased, and engaged in community life are ignored. These examples point to ways society minimizes the depth of their grief or ways that employers fail to provide them a time for bereavement.

LOSS

Loss is the diminishment of an ability, such as hearing, seeing, or tasting. The word *loss* is not an appropriate synonym for grief or bereavement.

Loss has become a frequent synonym for death for several reasons. Our culture chooses to deny the natural cycle of existence: birth, life, death. Today people have come to accept and expect the cycle to be birth, life—and then new, improved, and enhanced life. The intensity of this desire to deny reality is so extreme that it hinders people from even speaking the words *die, dead,* and *death. Loss* can become a euphemism for death—a way to avoid saying the word.

That's the reality that the young woman at the beginning of the chapter was pointing us toward. When people tell her they are sorry for her loss, she reacts negatively. Many others in the workshop nodded their heads in agreement when she mentioned her frustration at people saying, "I'm sorry for your loss." But one participant asked, "What are we *supposed* to say?"

Quickly, the class offered suggestions for alternatives: "I was sad to hear your dad died." "It was a shock to learn about your sister's death." "Your mom made the best brownies." "I was always envious of your brother's good looks." "When I read your uncle's obituary, it made me wish that I had known him better."

The kindest words are those that speak the truth in love. Often when we are bereaved, we say things like, "I feel like this is a dream, and soon I will wake up," or "I think I'm going to go in the house and see my loved one." When

27

family and friends simply say words like *death* and *died*, they are being gentle agents of healing. When we are in bereavement, people who speak the truth are a gift.

When someone expresses their genuine feelings regarding the death of our loved one, along with fond memories of the deceased, we feel less alone. We'll talk more about feelings later; for now, know that when you are the one giving comfort to someone else, they will be grateful if you can identify and voice your feelings about the death. It will let them know that they are not alone in their sadness, shock, numbness, or fear.

Weeks after my dad died, a coworker came to my desk and shared, "I miss seeing your dad and mom eating at Fuentes Mexican Restaurant. They always looked like they were having such great conversations and fun." I'm so grateful to this coworker for saying that simple thing. She, too, was missing my dad, and she gave me a wonderful picture of my parents.

After the death of a loved one, memories remain. For as long as memories stay alive, the dead stay present in our hearts, souls, and minds. Through shared anecdotes, the dead also take on new identities that may expand the living's appreciation of their character and personality.

MOURNING

To *mourn* is to regularly choose to respond to grief and bereavement in life-affirming ways. I began my studies and work in grief and bereavement in part because I received a Spirit-filled call to engage in life as a blessing to those who mourn so that they would be comforted.

You're holding this book, which is a concrete sign that you are in the process of mourning. This is a *giant* step, like one we took as children in a game of "Mother, May I?" It is an empowering step, because as soon as we choose to mourn, possibilities open to us.

For now, let's look briefly at the power and possibilities related to *choosing*. Thankfully, one cannot go far into this topic without learning about Viktor Frankl, Holocaust survivor and author of the classic *Man's Search for Meaning*. Frankl searched for the meaning of life and death while being held in four concentration camps. Left with the weight of these deaths on his heart, Frankl began to write his story, which he kept hidden.

After guards found his writing, they took him to stand before a tribunal. There he was stripped and forced to watch his writings burn. While there, a guard noticed that Frankl was wearing a band of gold on the fourth finger of his left hand. The guard demanded the ring. Frankl shared that as he reached down to pull off the wedding band, something happened inside of him. He said he touched a place inside himself that he would later call the last authentic "human freedom." Later he described what happened inside of him. "When we are no longer able to change a situation, we are challenged to change ourselves. Everything can be taken from a man but one thing: the last of the human freedoms." The last of freedoms, according to Frankl, is "to choose one's attitude in any given set of circumstances, to choose one's own way."

Notice that Frankl begins this reflection with "when." People usually choose mourning only after they have done everything within their earthly power to change the situation. You've prayed passionately or gone to professional counseling. You've read dozens of self-help books, spent time with career coaches, or traveled to get medical second opinions. You've tried alternative methods for healing, and you've kicked, screamed, and beat your head against the wall. Only when you finally accept that you are "no longer able to change a situation" can true mourning begin.

COMING TOGETHER

Finding a measure of peace in the face of raw grief can be a struggle. Whether it's anticipatory or disenfranchised grief, bereavement, or mourning, the work of grief is eased slightly when we recognize that we are not alone.

Stories like a Buddhist parable about a mustard seed remind us of this truth. It revolves around a woman named Kisa Gotami, who lived during the time of Buddha, when he had already achieved *nirvana* and was traveling to impart his teachings to others.

Kisa's only child, a very young son, had died. Unwilling to accept his death, she carried him from neighbor to neighbor and begged for someone to give her medicine to bring him back to life. One of her neighbors told her to go to Buddha, located nearby, and ask him if he had a way to bring her son back to life.

Bringing the body of her son with her, Kisa found Buddha and pleaded with him to help bring her son back to life. He instructed her to go back to her village and gather mustard seeds from the households of those who have never been touched by death. From those mustard seeds, he promised he would create a medicine to bring her son back to life. Relieved, she went back to her village and began asking her neighbors for mustard seeds.

All her neighbors were willing to give her mustard seeds, but they all told her that their households had been touched by death. They told her, "The living are few, but the dead are many." The woman returned home, sorrowing but not alone.

More recently, Elaine Gantz-Wright's neighbors and friends would have been more than willing to give her a mustard seed so that her son, Elliott, would come back to life. Sorrow continues to permeate the hearts of all who knew him. Elaine, knowing that she is not alone in her grief, shares in this excerpt from her essay "Grief's Fault" a portion of her processing of Elliott's death:

> Grief is a wilderness where you're disconnected from people, places, and purpose. It's difficult to make your way out of the wilderness because you're waist deep in the thicket and because grief clouds your mind's eye and scuttles your sense of direction. Nothing feels right. So many directions, but no place to go. It's visceral bewilderment—figurative and physical, together and apart, curious and terrifying. How could this have possibly happened?
>
> I'm finding it profoundly difficult to figure out where I am in the wilderness. I do see a line in the sand. I call it Grief's San Andreas Fault—forever dividing

the time before Elliot's death from the time after, but it also contains the seething stress of an imposing tectonic boundary. It's like I have two separate lives, two completely different identities—joined by a precarious fracture. And three years into my "after," I'm still brittle, directionless, and detached from most everything, except this unrelenting pain in my shattered heart. At least, the piercing icepick quality has morphed into a constant, dull ache. The anguish of grief never goes away. But I have to believe it will subside in time.

The other problem is that the edges of my life have shrunk into the circumference. Having spun myself into a tight emotional cocoon from the steely threads of grief, anxiety, and PTSD, I am making questionable professional choices—increasingly questionable, in fact. And as a single, seasoned, anxious mom, I have to make a living. It's a cruel conundrum.

So, what now? How do I make sense of this predicament in the phase of life—and somehow straddle the fault between Elliot's passing and my future? Caring pastors have advised, "Be gentle with yourself." That has always been a challenge for me, but I am noticing that grief is teaching me to take better care of myself through this worst of all possible times. To reparent Elaine in a way. So, this I know—for Elliot's death, for my younger son, Ian's, life and for my fragile soul, I want to live.

Emotional stories like this not only connect with our hearts; they also connect with our brains. Professor of psychology and neuroscience Uri Hasson notes that the activity in our brain actually starts to synchronize with the brain waves of the storyteller. Each story we read and hear connects us to others across time. These stories often motivate us to respond to our circumstances in ways we hadn't tried before. Recognizing the sorrow of others can plant seeds of truths during the process of grief.

SPIRITUAL PRACTICE

SAVORING THE WORD

Savoring the Word is an ancient method of prayer. It is often called *lectio divina*, which is Latin for "divine reading." This practice involves reading excerpts from holy texts or secular literature in a way that penetrates and changes not just our heads but our hearts.

Psalms and other portions of scripture are primarily used in the practice of lectio divina. In sermon preparation, I use this practice to experience scripture on a deeper level. In other times, I enjoy taking short, reflective essays, poems, and prayers so that the essence of the creative writing is savored word by word, phrase by phrase.

The method of lectio divina, in brief, is something like this:

• Set aside about fifteen to twenty minutes of quiet, uninterrupted time. Still yourself—or in the words of the great mystic Howard Thurman, "center down." You may want to use a breath prayer. This breath prayer is adapted from Viktor Frankl's reflections:

> **Inhale:** *Wisdom from on high and within,*
> **Exhale:** *Change me, my heart, my attitude.*

• Read the parable of the mustard seed or "Grief's Fault" earlier in this chapter; a scripture from your religious tradition; a poem; or a passage of prose that is meaningful to you. Remind yourself you are in God's presence. Read the passage again—preferably out loud. Then read the passage a third time, noting a word or phrase that stands out to you.

• Dwell on the word or phrase you noticed. How does it penetrate your heart? What feelings does it evoke? Does a memory surface? What image comes to mind? Notice how divine and inner wisdom are speaking to you personally about your life right now.

• Let your heart respond to this wisdom in prayer. Allow your words to form a prayer or mantra to carry with you today.

• Savor the silence in the presence of Wisdom, for even the power of words cannot capture the heart encounters you have experienced. Take time to write your prayer or mantra in a journal or an index card so that you may return to it.

• After engaging in this practice, reflect and write about your experience.

CHAPTER 3

WHY IS GRIEF EXHAUSTING? NAMING THE IMMENSITY

Hard work spotlights the character of people: some turn up their sleeves, some turn up their noses, and some don't turn up at all.

—Sam Ewing

One crisp fall evening, a woman arrived late to our next-to-last bereavement class. She was petite, and in previous gatherings, she had spoken demurely and with poise. Before taking a seat, she spoke with conviction salted with a pinch of disgust. "All I know is that my husband's death has highly inconvenienced me!"

Stunned silence hung in the air for a moment. Then came one burst of laughter, and then another, and another, until we were all doubled over. The truth of grief—in all its impolite and unorthodox ways of showing up—had been spoken.

I lifted a silent prayer of thanksgiving for these class members, their stick-to-it-iveness in the work of grief, and their honesty released and respected.

"Since his death, I've become a hermit," the woman continued. "I don't want to get out of the house—and then when I do, I don't want to go back home, because just seeing the garage door go up is painful. I want him to be inside the house, and I know he isn't. Oh, and I never knew grief involved so much *paperwork*!"

Groans of acknowledgment erupted around the room. "Quite frankly, I'm pissed off at God," she continued. "Our lives weren't supposed to end like this. I'm exhausted. All the time!"

And with that, she named another central truth of grief: it is exhausting. There are several theories about the exhausting work of grief, and they each hold merit. I say *work* because most people who have not experienced profound grief are clueless about the effort and energy— the *work*—required to move from an upended, miserable, often nonfunctional state of being to growing into an almost recognizable state of your former self.

How long does grief last? How long are we allowed to mourn? The standard bereavement policy of many employers will accommodate your experience of sadness after a loved one dies for three to seven days. For the most part, the public accepts displays of sadness for a very short period of time.

And bereavement in the wake of a loved one's death is, of course, not the only type of grief. What kinds of grief does the public accept—and for how long—after divorce, devastation due to natural disasters, diagnosis of a chronic or a life-threatening illness, or traumas such as combat duty, rape, and other forms of violence?

If a loved one has died, you know that there's no expiration date on grief. The kicker is that grief's invasion of your life is all-encompassing. If you're reading this book, you know this already: grief affects you physically, emotionally, socially, and spiritually. Not a single aspect of your life is off the hook.

EMOTIONAL AND PHYSICAL ASPECTS OF GRIEF

Many of us know that grief lives in our bodies. We are only now learning the extent to which that is true. But if grief lives in our bodies as well as in our emotions, it changes how we view the work of grief. How much do we, as a society, understand the connection between our emotions and our physical health? What grace are we willing to extend to people whose bodies are being changed by grief?

Ann Finkbeiner's *New York Times* essay "The Biology of Grief" describes the current challenges of researching the emotional and physical connections in grief. Finkbeiner is a science writer with a professional passion for discovering links between the emotions and biology of grief. She also became well acquainted with grief after her only child, Thomas Carl Colley, was killed in a train accident. "Right after he was killed," she writes, "I was in shock for a very, very long time." She thought that the grief process would be similar to what she experienced after the death of her father and that she would be OK. Then she started thinking, "Something's wrong with me because things aren't OK. And they are never going to be OK."

Finkbeiner became involved with Compassionate Friends, a support group for bereaved parents. Out of this "brave tribe," she interviewed thirty parents who had experienced the death of a child. She did this, she writes, as a way to show her son how much she loved him and to learn how other parents live and change through profound grief. *After the Death of a Child: Living with Loss through the Years* was published in 1998. Finkbeiner has combined her interest in science and her experience in grief. She says that the difficulty in research on grief is rooted in the fact that "grief is neither a disease nor is it classified as a mental disorder." And there are but a handful of researchers who straddle both fields.

Thankfully, some researchers are delving into the mechanics of grief and its impact on physical health. Two psychologists, Mary-Frances O'Connor at the University of Arizona and Chris Fagundes at Rice University, have discovered patterns that reveal that grief causes the brain to send a cascade of stress hormones and other signals to the cardiovascular and immune systems that can ultimately change how those systems function, over both the short and long term. Their research found that grief can have widespread impact on the heart and the immune system. There is also evidence stress related to grief can contribute to type 2 diabetes and some cancers.

While research is slowly emerging that confirms what we already know, traditional Chinese medicine has linked emotions to organs in the body for more than two thousand years. Anger seeks refuge in the liver, fear in the kidneys, joy in the heart, worry in the spleen, and sadness and grief in the lungs. This explains why so many folks are susceptible to bronchial infections with the onset of grief. Knowledge of this effect on the lungs led our nonprofit to first introduce breath prayers as a spiritual practice for comfort and health. Breathing deeply and praying while you're doing so can help you carry your grief, as we learned in the first chapter. It also helps your actual, physical body.

When we are in the process of grief, we often recoil at the intense emotional pain we feel. Sometimes we look for quick ways to numb or escape from the pain through use of alcohol or other drugs. The strategies we choose may be more or less harmful. Sleep and food, both necessary fuels that help our bodies avoid exhaustion, can be difficult to manage in grief. Some of us struggle with too much sleeping or too much eating, and others with too little.

The difficulty is due, in large part, to grief's obsession with making people and things disappear. In death, persons disappear. In divorce and other forms of grief, relationships evaporate into thin air, jobs vanish, and treasures burn or wash away in floodwaters, never to be seen again. It's the same with daily routines. Grief says, "Begone!"—and our habits disappear. Gone are patterns that ordered our daily living. And when our patterns are erased, a vacuum appears.

I'm guessing that you've tried to fall asleep with chaos quizzing you about the future. The questions are personal and difficult to hear. Some that have come to me are: When will you stop falling apart when you see that first star at night, knowing full well that your wish won't come true? Where is the place in this bed that used to be so comfortable? How will you pay the bills? What would you say or do differently if you could go back to your loved one's life for an hour?

Questions like these either keep us wide awake at night or wake us from unsettled sleep. The neon orange numbers on the clock shine 3:12. Much of the absence of routine, including sleep, is normal following grief. Yet there comes a time to seek professional advice and assistance.

One friend of mine waited six months to seek such advice. The psychiatrist listened in awe as my friend listed the numerous activities she had accomplished since the onset of grief. In a conversational lull, the psychiatrist said, "You are capable of doing many things in your grief. But you won't be able to function or do anything well without sleep." The doctor wrote a prescription for a thirty-day sleep aid, which helped my friend reset their sleep-wake cycle and find a routine again.

Sleep is crucial to functioning effectively, and it combats the exhaustion of grief. You can read the fine print of sleep studies (which may put you to sleep), or you can remember the advice another friend of mine received at the hospital following a heart attack. The doctor's prescription: exercise, no caffeine, no alcohol, no sugar, six to eight hours of sleep. And here's the clincher: if only one of these is doable, the doctor said, choose sleep.

Falling asleep and staying asleep is not difficult for me, and even in the days and weeks and months after my husband died, I slept fairly well, which I counted as a grace. But cooking for one? *That* has stirred up all sorts of things for me. I have found the self-discipline of balancing carbs and proteins and managing portion size to be very difficult. Sometimes I console myself by imagining that my friend's doctor is unfazed by the twenty pounds that have taken up residence on my short frame since my husband's death.

Linda, trying to find some balance in the throes of grief after the death of Archie, her husband, admitted to me, "I just eat ice cream right out of the carton. When I think I need some fiber, I throw a bag of popcorn in the microwave." Other people report that after a loved one dies, meals that used to bring them joy and comfort hold absolutely no appeal. Generally, people fall in one of two camps with regard to food and grief: *No Appetite* or *Bring It On!* Which food camp are you in?

Anthropologist Robin Fox says that food is paired with "a profoundly social urge." We share food in the company of family, friends, strangers, and larger communities. Studies show that socializing over food provides greater emotional and physical well-being. Shared meals feed individuals with the knowledge that they belong, and conversations often include encouragement, different perspectives on topics, and laughter. This emotional support promotes physical health in ways that alleviate stress, lower cholesterol, and reduce cardiovascular disease. When a person with whom we regularly ate meals dies, mealtime can become a fraught and sad endeavor.

There are too many links between sleep and food and grief to go into them in any depth in this chapter. But even just knowing that sleeping and eating are two of the ways that grief gets played out in our bodies might help us offer compassion to ourselves when we find ourselves struggling.

Sometimes when grief consumes people and patterns disappear, they become more prone to addictions. When someone tries to escape the work of grief through drug or alcohol use, they begin a cycle that seems at first effective and enjoyable. Once begun, however, that cycle is not easily broken. According to the National Council on Alcohol and Drug Dependence, "widowers over the age of seventy-five demonstrate the highest rate of alcoholism of any demographic group." Evidence shows that unresolved grief is the leading cause of addictions, and that substance abuse relapse is a sign of unresolved grief work.

SOCIAL ASPECTS OF GRIEF

Grief is often described in natural phenomena like waves in the ocean or in natural disaster terms. Sometimes grief is like an earthquake that sends aftershocks through our social lives. Grief changes social connections. While you and you alone are working through grief, your friends may be busy with their lives, not completely tuned in to what you're going through. That can be disappointing and disorienting. Meanwhile, acquaintances who have gone through something similar sometimes emerge as strong supports, carrying you along in ways you wouldn't have expected.

When her fortieth birthday rolled around, Marjorie Rose, the mother of one, made an appointment for her first mammogram. She was relieved that it wasn't nearly as painful and awkward as she had been led to believe. Her relief changed to worry, however, as the nurse asked her to wait for a few minutes, more minutes, and even more. The radiologist read the scan and scheduled additional tests.

The days waiting for a diagnosis were emotionally tortuous. Marjorie Rose wanted to know! She kept reliving previous trauma and griefs. Her father had died of melanoma days prior to her first year of college. Her mother had suddenly died a few years earlier, and she was still wrestling with the feelings of being an orphaned adult.

When the doctor finally diagnosed her with squamous ductal carcinoma in situ, she had to carry herself through weeks and months of treatments. The biggest surprise was the ways her social network changed. "Unexpected kindnesses from acquaintances and strangers were daily, and moms from my son's school kept us fed and our refrigerator stocked," she said. "But I kept wondering, 'Where are my bridesmaids?'" Her closer friends were less present to her than she would have hoped.

Sometimes the work of grief means noticing the disappearance of friends and family members. It may not be clear to us why they are protecting themselves from our grief, but it's better to acknowledge the additional sadness or anger this brings us rather than pretend that it doesn't hurt. Sometimes old friends and family *do* come through. Other times, through the process of grief, we meet new acquaintances and form friendships that would very likely not have had the opportunity to take root without shared grief.

Getting out and about socially takes courage after someone dies. And courage takes energy. Sometimes the path of ease is to become a hermit. Sometimes the work of grief means relying on the supports of old friends and family members. And sometimes the way includes drifting along murky waters with acquaintances and new friends who are in the same boat.

SPIRITUAL ASPECTS OF GRIEF

Grief can decimate or deepen our spiritual lives. It can dampen our faith or extend it into new dimensions. It can appear to do both, almost at the same time. Each time we experience the death of a loved one, friend, or colleague, we ponder our own mortality, too. Grief often prompts the most human and therefore most profound spiritual questions we can ask.

The impact of grief on our spiritual lives was made clear to me by a quote attributed to Pierre Teilhard de Chardin, SJ, a French Jesuit priest, philosopher, and teacher. It is said that de Chardin once said, "We are not human beings having a spiritual experience. We are spiritual beings having a human experience." Understanding our primal identity in this way—and recognizing grief as an inescapable human experience—frees us to explore our innermost thoughts and questions with both honesty and curiosity.

Much talk to God begins with the question "Why?" Job, that icon of loss and grief in the Hebrew scriptures, asks

"Why?" on behalf of all who experience grief. Frederick Buechner, theologian and author, wrote that God does not give us the whys of grief because it would be like trying to "explain Einstein to a little-neck clam." Furthermore, Buechner explains, God knows that "what Job needs isn't an explanation." Even if a divine explanation was given, Job would still have boils oozing with infection, his livelihood would still be lost, and his children would still be dead.

The question "Why?" is shorthand for the complete, confounded anguish the grieving feel toward the past, present, and future. We who have had a loved one die may ask how any divine, benevolent being can tolerate such anguish and tragedy or even allow it to exist. To work through such a spiritual crisis requires allowing ourselves to honestly rail against God. It means asking questions and then following them with sustained silence, listening for a holy response. Listening is the most difficult of communication skills. Listening is labor-intensive and calls for repeating the process multiple times. It is often helpful to practice with a professional counselor or spiritual director.

Listening and paying attention to our internal voice and to the divine voice is vital to our spiritual growth. The results of this lifelong work are tangible. Fleeting experiences of peace and compassion. Another byproduct is profound gratitude. After working through the harsh realities of grief, I discover that I am carried to a beautiful, wide-open place known as gratitude.

Since this chapter has been focused on the work of grief, the spiritual practice—nautilus renewal—focuses on a way to reflect on our own growth. Sometimes we can identify patterns only after a time of growth and change. The chambered nautilus is known as a "living fossil," because it has remained relatively unchanged during the past 450 million years. As a soft-bodied mollusk and distant cousin to squids and octopuses, the nautilus doesn't relocate to a new shell as it grows. Instead, it grows another chamber, and then another, and then another to hold its increasing size. With these distinctions, the nautilus is a symbol of nature's grace: in growth, expansion, renewal.

The chambered nautilus is a symbol of order amid chaos as reflected in its spiral precision, starting in the center and expanding outward. A variety of things in nature, from expansive to diminutive, embody this spiral formation: galaxies, hurricanes, sunflower seeds in the flower, cauliflower, and pinecones.

At the beginning of this chapter, Sam Ewing reminded us that grief work requires that we "roll up our sleeves" and get after it. You and your future are worth the work.

SPIRITUAL PRACTICE

NAUTILUS RENEWAL

This spiritual practice gives you time and space to rest and renew your heart and mind. As we meditate on the expanding spirals of the chambered nautilus, we may begin to see our own growth anew. You can use the drawing of the nautilus by coloring and writing in this book, photocopying the next page, or drawing your own.

- Set aside about fifteen to twenty minutes of quiet, uninterrupted time. If you have colored pencils, you may want to use them with this practice. Set aside several of your favorite colors. Begin centering with the breath prayer below.

> **Inhale:** *Holy, living breath of God*
> **Exhale:** *Renew my heart and mind.*

- Ponder what you yearn for or want to possess in fuller measure on your grief journey. What trait do you want to embody more often as you carry your grief? These might include attributes like courage, gratitude, joy, patience, peace, or serenity. Write the attribute inside your nautilus, at the beginning of the spiral. Let your mind wander. (No, you don't have to focus!)

- Now begin writing names of people in whose company you *feel* this attribute. You can write them along the lines of the shell.

- Expand the spiral formation by writing in places you have been where you *see* and *experience* this attribute. In what settings do you see yourself or others embodying this?

- Add colors and/or patterns that remind you of this attribute.

- When you are done, look at your nautilus and ponder it for a few moments. Reflect on your experience with the nautilus and write in a journal or notebook about any insights you gleaned about yourself or your grief journey during this practice.

CHAPTER 4

HOW DO WE RIDE THE WAVES? ENGAGING OUR SENSES

The five senses are the ministries of the soul.

—Leonardo da Vinci

When my great-aunt Mary died, my mom and I went to be with Mary's only child, Mary Alice. She was waiting for us at the threshold of her door—a wide-eyed adult orphan, fragile and trembling with fear. Mary Alice fell into my mother's arms and wept until she was too weak to stand. My mom eased her down to sit on the sofa.

As she wiped her tears, Mary Alice began to brighten up. Soon she was regaling us with tales of great-aunt Mary's childhood. She smiled as she told me about her mother's years as a bride adjusting to life on a West Texas ranch, located sixty miles from the nearest neighbor.

Halfway through one story, and then another, and another, the doorbell would interrupt Mary Alice. She would rise to answer the door, find a friend standing there, and then the scene that had played out with my mother— Mary Alice weeping, wailing, and nearly collapsing with sadness—would play out again. As soon as a friend visited a bit and then left, Mary Alice would regain composure and continue our story time.

As an eleven-year-old, I had never witnessed such tidal waves of grief. Watching her move from tears to smiles to tears once again, I was convinced Mary Alice was emotionally unstable—quite possibly, verging on the boundaries of "a little crazy." I shared my diagnosis with my mom on our way home, whereupon she replied, "That's how grief moves. It knocks you down. You get up. It knocks you down again."

Even if you know that grief is a wave, many people believe the waves are somehow predictable. It's easy to assume that the waves rise on special occasions—such as deceased loved ones' birthdays, anniversaries, and graduations. And the bereaved often do experience increased anxiety as these milestones approach; many even make detailed plans for how to cope when the day arrives. But others walking through bereavement remind us that living every day without their loved one is so painful that the "special days" are simply one more day without their loved one.

Whether the waves crash on an anniversary or on the most unsuspecting of Tuesday afternoons, they do share three things in common: a beginning, middle, and an end. Reminding ourselves of this pattern helps us ride the waves with greater measures of courage and confidence. We can regain some stability by assessing where we are in the wave's sequence.

Understanding this predictable pattern also helps us walk alongside friends who are riding waves of grief. Such knowledge can help us extend emotional generosity as we are better able to remain calm even when our friend is not. We know the wave will begin, crest with intense emotion, and then flatten out. Your steady presence will seal your friendship and serve as a deep well of support and solace for your friend.

Like snowflakes, leaves, and days, no two waves of grief are alike. They are unique. They take their different shapes depending on the source of grief and the attachments that have been disrupted or severed. Interestingly, waves of grief also take shape from our five primary senses—smell, hearing, vision, touch, and taste.

My abiding appreciation and respect for the importance of our senses in absorbing and processing life is due entirely to author Diane Ackerman. In her book *A Natural History of the Senses*, Ackerman writes, "The senses don't just make sense of life in bold or subtle acts of clarity, they tear reality apart into vibrant morsels and reassemble them into a meaningful pattern." Ackerman's reflection serves as an invitation to those of us whose realities have been torn apart by grief to activate our senses and receive the comfort and wonder they elicit.

Ackerman calls those who rejoice in sensory experiences as ways to discover the meaning in life *sensuits*. Those who have taken the Myers-Briggs Type Indicator may recall whether you naturally take in information through your Senses (the S type). It's quite possible that you've already been processing your grief as a *sensuist:* one who senses. Others, like me, who take in information iNtuitively (the N type) are encouraged to mindfully use our senses as we take in information and experience life. I promise your senses won't disappoint you and most likely will surprise you with ways to take next steps on your grief journey. We might say that sensuits, then, are those who give themselves over to their senses: to living with an awareness of the present as experienced through smell, taste, sound, touch, and sight.

In this chapter I suggest that we practice becoming grief sensuists: those who metabolize their grief by being attentive to the world and who find, in sensory experiences, a measure of healing or solace. Noticing and naming what we experience through our five senses is so crucial because, in grief, we sometimes long to withdraw and numb ourselves. Like Ron and his daughter, who we met in the first chapter, we often want to just move on. Strong memories, both happy ones and sad ones, are often triggered by our senses, and sometimes it's easier to turn away from memories than to engage them.

Love and grief are lived out in the minute moments of a day. Through practice, we can become more mindful of what we smell, taste, hear, see, and touch. This mindfulness will help us better ride the waves of grief and other emotions that follow in the wake of a loved one's death.

SMELL

Smell, perhaps because it is the first of our five senses to develop, evokes more intense and immersive memories than any other sense. It's sometimes known as "the mute sense," because it is next to impossible to describe how something smells to someone who has not smelled that scent. Helen Keller experienced the sense of smell as "a potent wizard that transports you across thousands of miles and all the years you have lived." These aromatic memories can both elicit waves of grief and assist us in riding those waves.

The second Christmas after my father's untimely death, Margaret, my niece, gave my mom an ornately wrapped package, hinting that it was purchased in the finest of stores. My mom carefully removed the ribbon and gift-topper so that she could use them for next year's presents. Then, deep in tissue paper, she found a bottle of my dad's signature cologne.

I knew little about the nature and dynamics of grief at this state of my life. I was irritated by the gift, which seemed insensitive. But by the time I had corralled my irritation for the sake of Christmas spirit, Mom had sprayed the room full of the cologne, with its citrusy notes, bitter-fresh rosemary, spicy lavender, and woody tones.

It was almost as if my dad had been resurrected. He seemed to sit among us—wearing his red Christmas vest, happy to have received a box of Anthony and Cleopatra cigars, and ready to assist in opening more gifts with his trusty pocketknife. Margaret had broken the silence of our grief by filling the room with aromatic memories so that we could breathe and speak healing stories of love and laughter. Our sense of missing my father didn't go away, of course, but that scent helped us ride the wave of holiday grief.

On a recent pastoral call, I was hit by a tidal wave of grief as the elevator doors opened in the living-with-assistance building where I was visiting parishioners. This time grief smelled of urine. The stench stifled my breathing, stopped me in my tracks, and transported me to other experiences with members of congregations I served. Grief swelled in my heart as I recalled vibrant saints of the church, pillars of the community, and quiet servants who had faithfully worked to bring the kingdom of God to earth as it is in heaven. I remembered those whose later years were marked by attendants washing, feeding, and clothing them.

Paralyzed by grief, I stayed in the elevator and pushed "G." I rode the wave to the ground level, where I rushed outside for fresh air and time to compose myself. I sat down on a nearby bench, closed my eyes, and took a deep breath. Tilting my head back, I slowly exhaled, taking another deep breath, and another, to clean out my airways.

I had been sitting there for only a moment when a subtle scent began entering my body. It piqued my curiosity. I opened my eyes and saw a row of abelias in bloom. Their rich, royal-like jasmine notes filled the air and my lungs with grace and beauty.

Before going back inside, I broke off several branches and breathed in deeply once again. Then I returned to visit the members of the church, carrying the branches of green leaves and soft white trumpet flowers. I made simple arrangements for their bedside tables, and I prayed that the sweet wildness of those scents would be a blessing.

TASTE

The meals we share with friends and family hone our skills as sensuists. Times around the table heighten our senses and often create sacred space—even when we're sitting with friends outside sharing nachos, burgers, fries, and holy-irreverent conversations. These meals renew our strength, give us different perspectives, push our sorrows toward abiding joy, and grant us measures of wisdom.

At the end of each six-week grief workshop that I lead, I invite participants to prepare their loved one's favorite dish to share with the group. We then gather around the dining table in my home. Cocoa and vanilla from someone's chocolate chip cookies compete with aromas of onions and peppers in spaghetti and chili. Before we eat, we give thanks for our time together, the loved ones we miss so much and whose deaths have led us to the group, and the buffet of their favorite foods. As we taste the food others have brought, we share stories about what made the dishes appealing, who prepared them, and when they were usually eaten. In the early days of each workshop series, knowing that our sharing was leading up to an evening such as this gave me the sustenance to reverently hold the grief each person shared.

The slow growth of wisdom through sorrow makes sages of us all. The word *sage* is from the Latin word *sapere*, which means "to taste." In its original form, *sage* was a verb: a process or a gesture by which we take in the world. The word *sage* implies that we make sense of the world and find wisdom by tasting. While watching and thinking may be helpful, actually *internalizing* what we experience, through our senses, opens us to wisdom. "Saging," then, is a fundamental process like breathing. When we "sage," we commit to listen with all our senses and all our being until listening becomes tasting.

When religious communities celebrate feasts and feast days of any kind—Christians celebrating the Lord's Supper, Jewish people observing the Passover—a shared meal takes on an even more sacred dimension. There is poignancy and power in these shared meals. The taste and the smell of foods connect us to memories from the past and helps us carry our sorrows in ways that connect us with those who have died.

SOUND

Yearning to hear a loved one's voice is a regular part of the grief process. What would you give to be able to engage in conversation with them again? To hear them tell you something—anything—about their day? Our longing to converse with our loved one who has died is often accompanied by a fear of forgetting the sound of that beloved voice.

Katie Krause, a friend, wrote an email to me describing such pangs of longing to hear her mother's voice:

> I could have a good day at work, meet the cutest dog at the park, get a gray hair, or just make my bed, and I would call my mom tell her all about it. She would act as interested as if I just told her I just met Queen

Elizabeth! Honestly, I could say the dumbest, most noninteresting things, and she would react and talk to me like she was so interested.

After all these months after her death, I still think, "I have to call Mom and tell her about that." A wave of grief hits me when I realize I can't. I can't physically call her. I immediately feel like someone just punched me in the gut. My stomach physically hurts.

It keeps hurting when grief reminds me that the sweet, happy, enthusiastic, and encouraging voice is no longer there. That voice that was so happy to hear about the egg I ate for breakfast or how a man cut me off in traffic on my way to work. Now it's just a memory. I know I can talk to her, but I can't hear her physical voice. I miss her.

Sometimes grief is simply the sound of silence. Sometimes it's the sound of someone else's voice or of music that our loved one listened to that reverberate into the depths of our souls and send waves of grief.

The sound of loved ones' voices is distinctive. I recall a theology professor mentioning that perhaps our loved ones' voice will be the thing we recognize when we meet again in our spiritual bodies.

The yearning to remember these voices often leads family and friends to keep voicemail messages from their loved ones. These messages are helpful when a wave of grief hits, and the ability to hear the loved one's voice provides comfort and a spiritual perception of their nearness.

TOUCH

Romantic embraces, friendly hugs, encouraging pats-on-the-back, tickling-of-ribs, passing-of-the-peace, firm handshakes, and playground wrestling: touch often returns us in our memories to earlier times. And we never outgrow it. While it is common to comfort babies and small children with physical touch and cuddling, we often ignore the need for physical touch in older children and adults. But the need for touch does not go away with age.

Grief, by nature, has an isolating effect. When we sit in ICU waiting rooms or stand in the hallway of a courthouse waiting for a sentence on our future or feel bewildered and devastated by natural disasters: in these moments, we need others to extend appropriate touches of solidarity, encouragement, and hope.

Through the sense of touch, Helen Keller not only survived but also thrived beyond all hope and imagination. She would put her hands on the radio to enjoy music. Through touch, she could tell the difference between cornets and strings. "She listened to colorful, down-home stories of life surging along the Mississippi from the lips of her friend Mark Twain."

During the pandemic isolation of quarantine and social distancing, I often thought of Virginia Satir, an author and psychotherapist recognized for her approach to family therapy. I found myself recalling her statement: "We need four hugs a day for survival. We need eight hugs a day for maintenance. We need twelve hugs a day for growth."

Each hug, lasting for twenty seconds for optimum effect, sends a well-being effect to the emotional hub of our brain. It's like sending a "peace be with you" message to our brain and body, which in turn lowers our anxiety. "More than 80 percent of respondents to one study in Sweden said hugging a stranger who was in mourning is appropriate."

An interesting practice related to touch, especially for those who enjoy fabrics and their distinct textures, is to name your feelings at the beginning, middle, and end of a grief wave. Then designate a fabric to represent each of those feelings. If we could feel fear outside of our bodies, for example, what fabric would best represent it? What about anxiety and sadness? Peace?

In a branding session for Faith & Grief Ministries, the artist asked me, "If a person could touch Faith & Grief, what would you want it to feel like?" I pondered the question while I imagined myself in a fabric store, walking up and down aisles and running my fingers across bolts of materials. After some pondering, I responded, "Cashmere."

Recall the first time and following days after word that a loved one had died. We felt an undeniable numbness and were grateful, although not fully aware, for the touch of others. Odd as it may sound, we're grateful that we are no longer numb even though we now feel pain in a variety of experiences. Our sense of touch can combat the pain. Ever run fingers through your hair or twist the tress around your finger? Ever seen men run their hand down the silk tie they are wearing? Ever noticed children carry a blankie that is in dire need of washing and yet even the strongest adult can't pull it away for a wash? Ever find that holding a book and touching the pages for a turn gives you a feeling of being grounded?

SIGHT

"Our language is steeped in visual imagery," Diane Ackerman observes. We make comparisons between objects and use phrases like "I saw it with my own eyes," and even when listening, we say, "I see where you are coming from."

Processing our own grief and observing people in grief are also steeped in visual imagery. Visitations, a tradition that is more infrequent with the increase in cremations, provided a time for family and friends to see the deceased one more time. Initial conversation around the deceased's body might sound like, "Oh, he looks so good. I can still see him sitting at the table playing solitaire, wearing that brown sweater with suede patches on the elbows. I really can't believe I won't see him anymore." We remember how our loved one looked, and our grief involves those memories.

Two years after Norwegian artist Edvard Munch's sister died, he painted "The Death Chamber." He paints the bedroom where his sister died, surrounded by her family, and he draws observers into the room, as well. From the way family members are sitting or standing, we can easily identify which one of them is "us" in the sacred sorrow. Munch is most known for "The Scream," which some believe may be a painting of himself. Through these two paintings, we have a brother-in-time, one who is insightful of the emotions and responses to grief.

HEIGHTENED AWARENESS

Riding waves of grief with a heightened awareness of our senses moves us to a deeper understanding of grief and of ourselves. And riding the waves as a sensuist takes practice. But that's the thing about grief, isn't it? The waves rise often enough for us to get plenty of practice!

When a wave of grief begins, pay attention to which of your senses it is activating. If it is your sense of smell, breathe deeply to open the tight pain in your chest.

If a memory of your loved one activates one of your thousands of taste buds, try to move your tongue over the grief. Determine if it is sweet, bitter, or salty. Do you want to savor the memory or spit it out?

Hearing the music and lyrics to a favorite song of your loved one—or perhaps one that seemed to have been written for the two of you—can bring on a capsizing wave of grief. Ride that wave out by recalling other songs your loved one enjoyed, or begin dancing to the beat by yourself.

As a wave splashes over me, I see my husband's magnetic and oh-so-photogenic smile. I hear his spontaneous mirth. The wave crests, and I feel him draw me near his body's warmth where my head nestles naturally over his heart. As the wave rolls to the shore, I'm aware that our embrace of touch is natural, comforting, and suspended in love. And I am filled with gratitude for my senses, which have slowed this particular grief wave's speed and force.

Learning about our senses and the ways they shape and impact our processes of grief is eye-opening (pun intended!). It's exciting to know that authors like Ackerman, persons interested in spiritual practices, and scientists are all captivated by the awakening of our senses to reduce stress, promote measures of comfort and delight, and discover more about how our emotions are formed.

Neuroscientist Lisa Feldman Barrett's research led her to write *How Emotions Are Made: The Secret Life of the Brain.* Barrett writes, "From sensory input and past experience, your brain constructs meaning and prescribes action." These are two important components in riding the waves of our grief. She adds that "With concepts, your brain makes meaning of sensation, and sometimes that meaning is emotion." The importance of identifying and processing our emotions (which now we know are shaped by our sensory input) is the focus of the next chapter.

This chapter's spiritual practice, object prayer, focuses on our senses of touch and sight. Such prayer has been available to persons for generations through praying with a rosary (Catholic or Protestant) or holding small icons, medallions, seashells, rocks, or other objects deemed as sacred. The practice helps replace negative emotions such as anxiety and fear with positive emotions of calm, peace, and comfort.

One research project, which worked with eight women and two men, discovered that praying with a sacred object gave participants "a sense of unconditional emotional support from the divine as well as guidance that helps them remain grounded as life falls apart around them."

Participants were asked to reflect on their experience of praying with a sacred object. One responded, "Wow. What's it like? Comfortable. A great love surge. Great happiness. Great joy. Great peace. . . . Deep. Deep peace, deep love, overwhelming love sometimes. I feel like crying now even thinking about it. . . . That's how important it is to me. I just know that [reaching God in this way] is what I must do."

Another noted, "The changes that happen when you meditate . . . are very, very gradual. You don't really notice them yourself. Other people might notice that you're more peaceful, more calm, more patient and kind."

Please keep in mind two things as you experience the spiritual practices in this book. You may prefer some more than others. That is to be expected. And note that practice is part of spiritual discipline, so you may want to try each one several times before making decisions about your preferences.

SPIRITUAL PRACTICE

OBJECT PRAYER

Over the centuries, object prayer has been a means to guide persons to feel closer to God and closer to loved ones, both living and deceased. The presence, significance, and weight of the object naturally moves your inner focus to an outward meditation of the object. Through this sensory prayer, memories and emotions may surface. Notice them. Ride their waves while holding your object. You are being held by the Holy One, who will not let you go.

For your first practice, consider choosing an item that was special to your loved one or that represents them in some way. In workshops and retreats that I have facilitated, participants have brought a wide variety of objects such as a father's shaving cup with soap and brush, a photograph, a piece of jewelry, a loved one's sweater that continues to hold her fragrance, and a family's favorite recipe card.

- Select an object that holds significance to you and can easily be held in your hands. It may be a sacred object or an object that belonged to your loved one or reminds you of them in some way.

- Center down with this breath prayer or one you use:

  Inhale: *Holy, Living God draw near*
  Exhale: *Touch me, heal me, comfort me.*

- Hold the object for several minutes, turning it over in your hands and engaging it with your senses. Come "in touch" with the meanings it holds for you. Look at its shape and color. Feel its surface and texture. If you chose an aromatic object, hold it to your nose and slowly breathe in its aroma.

- Put down the object and place your index and middle fingers on the side of your neck, near or on top of your carotid artery. Feel your pulse, and feel the living, beating presence of the Divine vibrating on your fingertips. Rest in this awareness.

• Pick up your object and continue holding it. Tell God your struggles. You might try out different ways of holding the object, including in the way that you imagine God would hold your struggles.

• Continue gazing at your object. Begin praying to be blessed by the promised hope and gifts that come through struggles.

• When you have finished your prayer, allow for a time of silence.

• At the end of your prayer time, record your experience. Consider how it felt to hold a sacred object as you prayed. How did holding the object enrich or diminish your prayers? How might you incorporate this practice in your future prayers?

CHAPTER 5

WHY DO OUR FEELINGS MATTER? BEFRIENDING OUR EMOTIONS

It is important to acknowledge all your feelings and not beat yourself up for having them.

Your feelings are not good or bad; they just are.

—Iyanla Vanzant

Wendy is a good friend of mine and one of the cofounders of Faith & Grief. During a time that we were both feeling weighted by grief, we decided to attend a weekend grief retreat together. We found one at a Carmelite monastery in California and signed up.

In that first evening class of the weekend retreat, our facilitator wasted no time in guiding us directly into grief's core. She handed each of us a crayon and a sheet of paper with five columns of words representing the spectrum of feelings associated with grief. These words included *abandoned, angry, anxious, bitter, boiling, brave, calm, confused,* and *crazy*—and those are just a few of the ABCs. Our assignment was to circle each word we felt or had felt in our grief.

"*What?*" one participant asked, surprised. "Nobody has ever asked me how I *feel*. They just assume I'm sad. And I sure didn't know there were this many feelings!"

Our facilitator, the epitome of calm, replied, "I'm glad you've now been asked. Take it slowly. Read each word silently and take note how your mind and body feel when you repeat it several times. If a word stirs a memory or if it jumps off the page and lands in your lap, circle it. Then I'll invite you to share some of the feelings that surprised you and which ones made you uncomfortable to circle."

We slowly went through the list and circled our feelings. Then we were eager to share. When everyone around you assumes that grief only looks like sadness, it can be incredibly liberating to be given words for the other ways that grief is known.

"It's anger!" one woman exclaimed. "I never knew I could explode with anger until my husband died. Maybe it was closer to rage. My adult children were shocked and speechless. They had never seen me in such a state of emotional turmoil." She told us about an evening soon after her husband died. It was the evening before her adult children had to return to their homes, and they had decided to order from their favorite Chinese restaurant. Her two sons volunteered to take everyone's orders. "It all got rather complicated with some wanting brown rice, others fried, and still others wanted white rice," she told us. "I told them that I liked any kind of rice and to order me anything but chicken. I even said, 'No chicken!' right as they were walking out the door. Well, sure enough, when the boys got home and began opening all the orders, every single one of them—all twelve—had chicken! Chicken this, chicken that, chicken, chicken, *chicken!*"

Our new friend's eyes were bright, and her face was animated. She was such a great storyteller that by now half of the class was laughing.

"I exploded!" she continued. "I was so angry. How could they have done that? I let the entire family have it. I can still see them all staring at me in disbelief at my outburst. I stormed off to bed and had a good cry."

That story broke the dam of pent-up feelings for the rest of us. We shared. We listened. We connected on a soul level. We all agreed that anger often accompanies grief. In fact, as we learned that weekend, grief doesn't always feel like sadness at all. Sometimes, as our new friend taught us, grief looks like being mad at your kids for bringing home chicken. It can even sound like laughter.

All our feelings matter—even the ones that don't make a lot of sense at the time. Learning more precise words for our emotions—and then befriending them—is part of the work of grief. As we name our emotions, we make them known, and we invite them to speak. All emotions, with their variety of names, will continue to resurface until they receive acceptance. Emotions, like people, want to be respected and acknowledged by name rather than ignored, spoken about with sarcasm, or made into the butt of a joke. Let's look at just a few emotions that often surface in times of bereavement.

ANGER

Anger has many names: miffed, pissed, furious, enraged. My dad liked to use "sorely vexed." Anger is often called a secondary emotion. This doesn't mean that it is less important than other emotions; rather, it means that anger never arrives in a vacuum. It's the unseen, one mental health professional told me. It's the buried emotion we haven't been willing to face. Anger is embedded in our primitive need to live and protect ourselves against outside aggression and inner pain or trauma.

Many people in grief admit that our most intense anger is directed at God. Depending on the image of God you grew up with, being angry with God can be scary. (What if we're struck by lightning? Or thrown in the belly of a whale?) But we can remind each other that our anger is justified. God has not answered our prayers for a miracle. God has not intervened to change the circumstances to give us what we need and most desire. And God has not awakened us one morning with the good news that our grief was only a bad dream.

At that retreat, we all began to share ways we had come up with to release anger. Ideas included:

- throwing ice cubes at a fence
- signing up for kickboxing
- pulling every weed invading our flower beds
- rolling up a newspaper and beating it on a mattress
- screaming when alone in the car

Add your own to the list. What do you do to release anger?

Recently I drove to an ATM to get my monthly stash of twenties. After completing the transaction and ready to back out of the space, I failed to look in my rearview mirror and rolled gently into a car that was parked behind me. Chagrined, I jumped out to see what damage I may have caused. Thankfully, there was none.

The owner of the car came storming out of the ice cream shop next door, his waffle cone piled high, and began verbally accosting me. I apologized, but I doubt he could hear me. His vitriol and stream of anger flowed with four-letter words. His twenty-year-old car had never been hit, he screamed repeatedly. I stood there, frozen in shock.

Finally, he said, "You stupid c&@#, just get the hell out of here."

I'm not sure what got into me next. But before I knew it, I had pulled out the phrase we say to each other in church. "Christ be with you," I replied, as I walked back toward my car.

Stepping closer, he said, "*What* did you say?"

I turned and repeated myself.

"Well, Christ be with you too, you motherf★&%@er!" he responded. "Because you're going to need him."

"I am truly sorry that I tapped your car," I said as he headed toward his car. "I am also sorry that you are going through so many challenges in your life."

He slammed his car door and roared out of the parking lot while I stood there, trying to catch my breath. A deluge of thoughts swirled in my mind. I was relieved he didn't have a gun, and I was glad Christ was with me and also with him. And I even felt a bit of gratitude that I could make some degree of sense out of this man's anger. I wondered what pain or grief he must be carrying. I wondered if someone close to him had died and whether he felt helpless in the face of it. And I prayed that someday he would be able to acknowledge and name it.

HELPLESSNESS

Ironically, anger has the capacity to make us believe the myth that we are in control of our lives. Anger is a cover-up for our sense of helplessness. We are frequently helpless in the face of circumstance: if someone loves us, whether a loved one stays alive, how others respond to circumstances, if employment policies are fair, or if random acts of violence, injustice, or terminal diseases occur. And that's just to name a few.

When a loved one dies, we may feel more helpless than we ever remember feeling before. Some of us even struggle to type the word *helpless* because we so strongly resist feeling that way (and by "some of us" I mean me). Anger is easier.

Occasionally I stand in front of a mirror and ask out loud: "Am I angry, or do I feel helpless?" I've been surprised how many times I have realized that I feel helpless rather than angry. When we acknowledge we are helpless, it is neither an excuse nor a dismissal of grief. Even when I feel most helpless, I can still make responsible choices, and I still need to process my grief. An acknowledgment of my helplessness is actually a surrender to the truth, which empowers me to act wisely.

Naomi Oh, in her essay, "A Posture of Surrender," describes my sense of surrender's empowerment. She writes, "When I choose to surrender, I feel my world expanding. There is more space in my mind and a greater sense of abundance rather than scarcity. Instead of narrowing in on isolated moments with scrutiny, I look at the big picture. I imagine an expanse of possibilities and not simply just the challenges I must endure. I give myself permission to rest and be fully present in pain and discomfort."

In grief, our world does become smaller. This may be a gift of grace, because we couldn't handle anything larger. Yet I agree with Naomi Oh that it is helpful and healthy to "look at the big picture" or at least spend some time in our state of surrender to imagine and dream of possibilities that may be incubating in our helplessness. Surrender, says Oh, "is not the absence of uncertainty [or helplessness], but rather, the act of holding space for it."

FEAR

"Fear cripples us more than any disease ever could. It takes eminent good sense and turns it to gelatin," writes Joan Chittister. The shock of death, whether sudden or anticipated, means fear reverberates through our bodies. If *this* can happen, what *else* can?

Teal's husband died from sudden cardiac arrest while driving to work one morning, leaving her as a single parent to their two children. In the days that followed, Teal found herself returning items she had recently purchased for refunds; with the sudden loss of her husband's salary, which reduced the family income by more than half, she was deeply concerned about being unable to financially support her children.

Emotions rarely visit our hearts one by one. They enjoy company, and so they usually come in pairs or even groups. Under typical circumstances, we aren't aware of the dynamics between our emotions. After a parent's lengthy illness, a participant asked, "How can I feel both sad and relieved?"

Awareness of the comingling of emotions helps us understand why our stomachs may feel tied in knots throughout the process of grief. When taking an emotional inventory, I ask myself, "Am I mad, sad, glad, or scared?" On occasion, my response is, "Yes, all of the above." These combinations of emotions occur in both younger and older persons. After her husband died, a woman who had sold her home of fifty-five years and her ten-year old Honda on the same day shared, "I was so relieved! I wanted to buy champagne and celebrate with my friends. At the same time, I was exhausted and sad. Moving is so hard and a little scary. Since I'm grieving, it's even more than scary. I'm afraid I won't be able to adjust to living in this retirement community without my husband and with so many people."

After the death of his wife, C. S. Lewis wrote *A Grief Observed* under the pseudonym M. W. Clerk because he did not want to be identified with the raw emotions shared in the book. "No one ever told me that grief felt so like fear," Lewis writes at the beginning of the book. "I am not afraid, but the sensation is like being afraid. The same fluttering in the stomach, the same restlessness, the yawning. I keep on swallowing."

SHAME

Shame grows out of the negative feelings about *who you are*. Other feelings, like guilt, are about *what you do*. Seeds of shame are planted in childhood experiences of being abused physically or emotionally or being judged on appearances rather than authenticity. Notice the emphasis and repetition of *being*. Our very being is often filled with shame that *others* have caused. Not one of us is *born* full of shame.

Grief shame occurs when others ridicule or humiliate you for not grieving enough (the way they think you should) or not grieving at all. In an essay for *Huffington Post*, Tim Lawrence writes, "A dear friend is killed in a car accident. A few months later, I don't feel that I've sufficiently 'gotten over it' and people start telling me to move on. So I hide my grief, push my chin up and allow the cataclysm inside of me to tremble in perpetuity."

Grief shame may also be imposed on a person because they cannot or do not grieve the death of an abusive parents, spouse, or child. One such person was blessed to encounter Rabbi Shawn Zell, a compassionate rabbi, who understood. Zell wrote a prayerful poem that begins, "I wish I could bemoan the void in my life / Now that you are gone, *but I cannot.* / I can, however, help fill the lives of others / By putting a smile on their heart." (The full prayerful poem is in the resources section at the end of the book.)

Lawrence also notes, "While there are many reasons people feel they cannot grieve, shame is the most disabling. We are besieged with shame in our grief journeys, and we do everything we possibly can to hide it. The most horrific aspect of shame is that it's silent. You don't really *see* it. It is a silent killer." Shame is seen, heard, and diminished when we open ourselves to our vulnerabilities and to our authentic stories.

The variety of roots of shame make it difficult to name and untangle when it appears in grief. Seeking wisdom from professionals is especially beneficial if grief evokes feelings of shame or you are grief shamed. Very likely, it has taken years for your identity to be wrapped up in what others think and how you have been treated. Through professional help, prayer, and spiritual disciplines, a moment of time will come, a flash of divine light will shine, and truth will begin singing that you are loved for who you are.

GUILT

While those of us living within Western religious or secular cultures do not typically befriend our anger, helplessness, fear, or shame, many of us do gravitate toward guilt. Guilt may be the top emotion that people own. People feel guilty about procrastinating on actions regarding health, relationship, and employment issues. After a loved one dies, those who remain often feel guilty about having stepped over boundaries and having said too much. Or they feel guilty that they didn't say "I love you" or "I'm sorry" or "I forgive you." Why does guilt seem to relish appearing in the grief process?

Our culture prizes *doing*. Therefore, when there is nothing that can be done—when we can't halt the metastasizing of cancer cells or the speeding of a car through a red light— those of us who remain will often *do* guilt. Paradoxically, we almost feel better when we do guilt, even when we had no power over what occurred. A friend admitted, "When I feel guilt, I at least feel in control. I'm doing *something!*" The problem is that doing guilt doesn't get us anywhere. Guilt is like being stuck in a revolving door. We keep going round and round, faulting ourselves.

When we talk about our feelings of guilt in the wake of a loved one's death, friends may respond, "But you *shouldn't* feel guilty." Or they shut down the conversation by saying, "You don't need to feel guilty." Such responses only encourage us to make a more definitive case for feeling guilty—which simply keeps us stuck in the revolving door.

A caring friend who knows enough about the weight of grief can sometimes lead us out of the revolving door by saying, "Tell me more about your guilt." They care enough about us to keep listening to us as we process the raw or lingering grief. Chances are that, in talking, we will acknowledge other feelings too.

YEARNING

Now it's time to acknowledge an emotion that is soft-spoken and shy in nature, content to dwell in the soft light. Yearning is its name. *Sehnsucht*, its German alias that cannot be fully translated into English, may better describe it. *Sehnsucht* represents the wistful desire for an ideal alternative. It is the homesickness that taps our hearts, the melancholy that slips into occasions of joy, or the longing for previous moments. When a loved one dies, yearning is central.

Yearning is inextricably linked to the human condition, and in grief its size and intensity increases. A man yearns to relive the last twenty seconds of his wife's life—surely, he would have kissed her one more time. A young woman who mourns the death of her premature child wanders the produce section of the grocery store, weighing cabbages. She yearns to find and hold one that weighs one pound, seven ounces, the weight of her child. A child aches to know what heaven is like since he has been told it's his grandfather's new home. In the abyss of our grief, we yearn for all that we cannot have.

Yet somehow sorrow has a way of becoming an unbidden gift of spiritual growth and self-understanding. Our yearnings are the sighs or groans that articulate our highest and deepest abiding values—our joys, our meaningful connections, our loves.

THE AWAKENING HEART

The death of a loved one becomes a line in the sand of our time on earth, or what writer and consultant Elaine

Gantz-Wright, whose adult son died, calls "grief's fault," in the excerpt from her essay that you read in chapter 2. Grief's fault is a line that clearly demarcates a *before* and *after* in our living and self-understanding. In this *after* time, we have a plethora of opportunities to learn and appreciate new ways of being and understanding through different traditions and faiths.

For instance, Buddhists guide our attention to the word *remorse*, which has the power to transform. They believe that we are filled with remorse when our "awakening heart" recognizes that we have caused pain to others and ourselves by acting in ways that are diametrically opposed to our true nature. How many times have we asked ourselves, "*Why* did I say that?" or "I *should* have spent more time with them or at least called them." or "I *wish* I could have that moment back." In this awakening, a door of our heart opens to an invitation: to vow that the next time such a circumstance arises, we will choose to act according to our higher angels. The feeling of guilt convicts us, while the humble feeling of remorse transforms us.

A different type of "awakening heart" occurs when we look back over our lives and recognize that what we thought was a major grief or curse has somehow become a spirit-filled gift or blessing. This gift of providential care sometimes reveals itself in technicolor in my life. And I've heard stories of the way it appears in the lives of others.

A woman and her mother wept in my office because her wedding was called off at the last minute. Several years later, this same woman was radiant as she introduced me to her fiancé. "Someone," she said, pointing upward, "was definitely looking after me!"

A group of siblings woke up to the unexpected news that their father had died that morning. As we were planning the memorial service, the older brother turned his head toward the ceiling and seemed to be in deep thought. "What are you thinking?" a sister asked. "I just remembered what dad used to say. He'd say, 'When I die, I hope I die in the morning rather than working all day and then dying at night.' This memory of hearing him say that makes his death a little more bearable."

These "awakenings of the heart" are examples of gratitude. Gratitude is the one emotion that cannot be self-directed. It cannot be imposed or forced on us, for that would hold the seeds for resentment. Gratitude also refuses to be an expectation. I still remember the shocked look on a trusted colleague of mine when I said in exasperation, "I'm sick and tired of being grateful." That honest statement turned out to be an antidote—one that, ironically, served to awaken my heart to gratitude.

I discovered rest when I quit *looking* for things for which to be grateful and let the eyes of my heart begin *noticing* things around me. I recognize that these two ways of seeing sound like one and the same; however, they are quite different experiences. We notice expressions of an adult child identical to our dead mother. We notice when people let us talk and refrain from finishing our sentences or giving us advice. We notice the dances of light from birthday candles. We notice our heart awakening with gratitude.

Surprisingly, I have discovered that at times I can even be grateful for my grief. Grief highlights, underscores, and even magnifies the people, moments, and things that I had noticed and now treasure. Lines from Kahlil's Gibran's prose, "On Joy and Sorrow," from *The Prophet* brought this awakening of the heart to me: "Your joy is your sorrow unmasked. . . . When you are joyous, look deep into your heart and you shall find it is only that which has given you sorrow that is giving you joy. When you are sorrowful look again in your heart, and you shall see that in truth you are weeping for that which has been your delight."

BEING YOURSELF

We cannot conquer grief. Perhaps that's why we sometimes try to hide from it, thinking it is self-protection. We'd rather do activities we can hone or achieve or get good at. Going through grief is not like learning to tie our shoes or grill a steak to perfection. Instead of aiming to "succeed" at that which cannot be mastered, we can recognize that in each grief we experience, we are both novices and professionals.

We are novices because every grief is different. The death of a parent is different from that of a child or spouse. The experience with one type of grief doesn't serve as a paradigm for another. So every time we go through bereavement, we experience something new. At the same time, we are also "professionals" in our grief, in that no one can tell us how to grieve. We are the experts on our own process, even if we don't always feel like we are. We have become accustomed to the wave pattern of our own emotions. We have learned, or are learning, to identify the ebb and flow.

Every grief is personal and presents its own context; our family and friends will most likely grieve the same unwelcome event in different ways. Such differences can cause significant disharmony, because one or more persons in the group think everyone else should be acting, feeling, and responding in identical ways. But that can't happen. Chances are that no two people are going to feel and react in grief the same way. Be you.

What *can* take place is honoring and respecting each other's individual emotional responses. If you're anything like me, you may need to remind yourself of this truth more than once to bring your blood pressure down. Knowing that the waves of grief will hit you differently than they hit someone else can stave off our tendency to assume that everyone will grieve the same way we do. As Henri Nouwen writes, "When we honestly ask ourselves which person in our lives means the most to us, we often find that it is those who, instead of giving advice, solutions, or cures, have chosen rather to share our pain and touch our wounds with a warm and tender hand."

If, in your process of grief, you find yourself swallowing your feelings or stuffing down hopelessness or despair day after day after day, be mindful that you may be experiencing situational depression. Depression gets its name because feelings are *depressed* rather than expressed. If you think you might be depressed, it's time to get help.

You may find it helpful to visualize your feelings as being contained in a large, covered soup pot. Regularly, you need to slowly lift the lid to check to see how things are simmering. Don't wait until your emotions boil over, creating a mess of pain and suffering that could be averted by seeing a spiritual director or professional counselor and joining an ongoing grief support group. Of course, I recommend Faith & Grief groups, which can be found at faithandgrief.org and are offered online and in person. Emotions will continue to resurface until they are given the respect they deserve, the understanding they long for, and the challenge of growth they can provide.

SPIRITUAL PRACTICE

RAIN MEDITATION

When you experience an encounter with another person or an emotion that leaves you feeling ambushed or blindsided, pulled away or detached, or simply thoroughly discombobulated, find some time to engage in this spiritual practice.

Michele McDonald, cofounder of Vipassana Hawaii, coined the acronym RAIN for a Buddhist meditation and mindfulness practice that can help you be mindful of your emotions in any given situation. Tara Brach, in her work on self-compassion, popularized it further. RAIN stands for recognition of what is going on; acceptance of the experience versus ignoring or denying; investigation, with interest, of what is happening; and nonidentification, in order to look at the experience objectively rather than personally.

Since grief work is replete with a wide range of emotional experiences, becoming familiar with this practice and including it in your repertoire of meditations can help you befriend your emotions.

- Prepare your heart, soul, and mind to meditate with this breath prayer or one you prefer.

> **Inhale:** *Holy One, give me wisdom to see*
> **Exhale:** *my grief as you see it.*

- *Recognize* what just happened by noticing the *who*, *what*, *when*, and *where* the experience took place as well as your feelings that surfaced and are now receding.

- *Accept* your feelings. They are valid; they are real! You are a spiritual being full of emotions.

- *Investigate* ways your feelings are making themselves known in your body. Is your jaw clenched? Shoulders slumped? Cheeks flushed? Each time you locate a feeling, repeat the breath prayer, and imagine your breath flowing through that location until the feeling begins to subside. For example: breathe through the muscle tightness in your jaw. Repeat this practice for each location.

- *Not identifying* is a tricky step that holds possibility for fun and challenge. This is also sometimes called "natural awareness." Take on a new identity. Rather than being the *participant* in this experience or emotion, become an *observer*. You may want to try to see the experience like God or a loving bystander would see it. What new things do you notice? Observe the experience as if had happened some distance away from rather *inside* yourself. This distance is a space of freedom.

• Reflect on this four-step meditation and write about your thoughts. Which step was easier? Which was more difficult? Why? How would you describe RAIN meditation to a friend? If it becomes a helpful practice and you would like to know more about it, find out more in *Wide Awake* by Diana Winston and *True Refuge* by Tara Brach.

RECOGNIZE | ACCEPT | INVESTIGATE | NOT-IDENTIFY

CHAPTER 6

HOW DO WE TAKE CARE OF OURSELVES? EXPRESSING SELF-COMPASSION

If your compassion does not include yourself, it is incomplete.

—Jack Kornfield

The recession of the early 1980s was one of the most severe economic situations since World War II. My first husband and I owned an office supply store during that time. We managed through the early years by selling furniture, double-entry ledger books, and mechanical pencils. But after the recession, local businesses turned to wholesale retailers for their low-priced supplies. Day after day after day, I was filled with stress-infused grief from watching our business sink deeper into debt. I tried not to dwell on our dire circumstances, but the anguish was unrelenting. I worried during the day and had nightmares when I slept.

In pursuit of emotional relief, I began a daily ritual. I would slip out of bed before the break of dawn and make my way to my favorite green chair. For twenty minutes, I would focus only on my worries: my dashed hopes of owning and operating a successful business, my fears of financial ruin that made corporate and personal bankruptcy appear imminent, and my embarrassment of failure. I'd offer to God my fears and tears as a prayer of lament.

Throughout the day, then, anytime feelings of doom or failure would interrupt my work, conversations with friends, or times of delight with my children, I would address those feelings head on. "I'll spend time with you tomorrow morning," I'd say to my worries in my head. "Don't interrupt me now."

Before I began my mornings this way, I would spend so much energy trying *not* to think about my negative feelings that I would be worn out and despondent by evening. The exertion of energy was like trying to push a beach ball below the surface of ocean waters: impossible!

But what *was* possible for me, and what can be possible for you, was to begin offering myself compassion. Years later, a friend approached me after what I call a "zig-zaggy day": a day of emotional highs and lows. It had been a day full of pastoral care, and of attending to other people's needs. With compassionate directness, my friend gave this memorable instruction, "Fran, take care of yourself. Nobody else will."

On days when I recognize that I'm running on empty and times when it's clear that I'm maxed out, I hear my friend's words of advice and reality. Nobody else can give you self-compassion. To show ourselves compassion, we must answer some foundational questions: What is compassion? What is *self*-compassion? What makes self-compassion difficult? Why is it important? And what does all this have to do with grief?

THE PLATINUM RULE

Compassion is the combination of two words: *com*, "with," and *pati*, "to suffer." So compassion, to "suffer with," fills us with a desire to relieve suffering and moves us to take such action. The principle behind this ethical behavior is the belief that human beings are interconnected to such a degree that when one suffers, we are moved to *suffer with* and actively participate in relieving or reducing the suffering.

The world's major religions all revere compassion, as seen in the Golden Rule: *Do unto others as you would have them do unto you.* Self-compassion calls for us to turn the rule's wording and understanding on its head: *Do unto yourself; then do likewise unto others.* Perhaps this new wording and understanding should be called the Platinum Rule. Let's read and ponder this Platinum Rule again: Do unto yourself; then do likewise unto others.

You may have involuntarily flinched when you read the Platinum Rule. The spontaneous reaction could stem from never taking your needs and desires seriously. So many individuals in caregiving professions are "other focused" and have little to no experience *receiving* care. What would their care of others be if they first cared for themselves?

On a deeper level, you may have flinched because you've never grasped the intense love and desire God has for *you* to *be* and *become*. The greatest influences in my life have come from men and women who by grace, faith, doubts, and renewed faith believe they are loved by the Creator of all life. Such belief has in turn filled them with an abundance of love for others. So if you flinched, hang in there for a moment. Keep reading and, if you can, let yourself feel an open curiosity toward God's unclaimed love and grace.

My Sunday school teacher when I was in junior high used the acronym JOY to make her lessons memorable. She would assure my class that this fruit of the Spirit—joy—was available to us if we loved Jesus first, others second, and yourself last. After all, didn't Jesus say, "And a second [commandment] is like [the first]: You shall love your neighbor as yourself"? Maybe you received similar lessons too.

Throughout my years serving in pastoral care, I met with people who had followed this lesson. Throughout their lives they had put Jesus first, others second, and themselves—well, they'd put themselves dead last. They would come to my office and vomit words of self-condemnation like: *I'm not good enough. I should have done more. I get so mad at myself when things don't go according to plan.* They'd express resentment and despair: *Why should I even bother with this? No one is appreciative of all that I have done.* They'd close their eyes and say, as if it were a prayer of confession: I'm just so exhausted.

I would wait until their eyes opened, and then I would say, "I can well imagine that you feel exhausted. What act of kindness could you do for yourself today?"

They'd look at me like I had just spoken to them in Latin. I would repeat the question: What kindness could you offer to yourself today? Still, most of them seemed to be at a complete loss. "Wouldn't that be selfish of me?" some would say. "Aren't I supposed to put others before myself?"

Together, then, we'd ponder the following question: How can we give compassion and kindness to others if we're in short supply or empty of these things ourselves?

In her book *Fierce Love*, Reverend Dr. Jacqui Lewis describes *ubuntu*, a Xhosa word from South Africa that means, essentially, "I am because you are." Ubuntu recognizes the inner worth of every human being—starting with yourself. Ubuntu prompts us to consider what our world would be like if human beings first accepted and filled their hearts with God's love, compassion, and kindness for themselves—and then shared the contents of their hearts with others. To emphasize the far-reaching ethics of ubuntu, Lewis entitles chapter 1 of *Fierce Love* "Love Yourself Unconditionally: It All Starts Here."

Striving for perfection renders us unable to accept these God-given gifts for ourselves and makes us incompetent in practicing self-compassion. We struggle between our desire and inability to self-generate, earn, or win these gifts. Such ongoing struggles produce a chatter of self-criticism, self-loathing, and unworthiness. These struggles deplete our energy and drain us of compassion for ourselves. Dr. Kristen Neff, a pioneering researcher in self-compassion, helps us understand this inner chatter comes from ignoring our feelings. Recognizing our feelings, therefore, is an act of self-compassion. She suggests cultivating self-compassion in a similar manner as we practiced befriending our feelings in the previous chapter. The benefits of cultivating self-compassion are especially helpful in the grief process.

Neff cites studies that conclude self-compassionate individuals are more interested in learning goals rather than performance goals. "People with learning goals are motivated by the desire to develop new skills and master tasks," she writes, whereas "people with performance goals are motivated to achieve primarily to defend or enhance their ego . . . and feel they must do better than others to feel good about themselves." In grief, we learn, right off the bat, that there is no way to "do better" than someone else, and no steps to tick off. There is, however, much to learn about the nature and dynamics of grief and ourselves in the process.

When my husband served as an academic dean at a seminary, he encountered many performance-driven students. He good-naturedly described them as students looking for a donkey to ride through some town. When one student received a B in his worship class, the student came to his office and fell in a heap because the student had never received a grade lower than an A. After much folderol, Bob led the student to the registrar's office where he changed the B to an A and said, "Now perhaps you can focus on learning."

There are no grades in grief. There's no honor roll. We simply plug along, taking one day, or even one hour, at a time. Yet with every story spoken and heard, insight gained, and spiritual discipline practiced, we develop our grief skills and become more confident with our intuitions. There's no performance here, only learning.

Neff writes that "studies indicate that another gift of self-compassion is that it fosters a growth rather than a fixed mindset." Psychologist Carol Dweck coined these terms. A fixed mindset is one that assumes that traits like intelligence are basically inherent and unchangeable. If you have a growth mindset, you believe that people can grow and improve through effort and over time. With this book in hand, you've acknowledged that you're curious about the spirituality of grief, you're open to possibilities and ways of navigating the journey of grief, and you're keenly aware that life, including every bit of you, is not fixed. We are dynamic beings capable of growing. When I was getting my divorce, I desired to grow better rather than become bitter through the grief. I feel the same way since Bob's death.

Sadly, persons with a fixed mindset who believe that there is nothing positive they can do in the grief process may be the ones who live out their lives in denial or avoidance at all costs. If or when they do speak of their grief, they usually throw up their hands signaling defeat and say, "It is what it is." Part of that is true. Yes, our loved one has died. We cannot change that fact. Another part of it is false. We can unravel the tangle of emotions that are making it difficult for us to swallow, sleep, or see hope, and we can name them one by one. We can befriend them with compassion.

"Self-compassion not only fosters the belief that growth is possible, it also increases our ability to work for it," writes Neff. We are already aware that grief is work. And work takes energy. If we fall into the trap of self-criticism, we use up all our energy. We become worn-out defeatists. Yet even when practicing self-compassion takes some focus, it's worth it.

Another way to state the Platinum Rule is to love others the way that God loves you. So while we shouldn't throw out the Golden Rule, we may need to sometimes turn it on its head or change its direction. We can only love as much as we have experienced love ourselves. We love as we are loved.

Over the years, I've been privy to the joy of grief workshop participants and friends who began practicing self-compassion. After the death of her husband, a bridge buddy purchased a sofa covered in flowers that resembled Monet's garden. At the beginning of their marriage and while they reared two sons, sofas were always jewel-tone plaids or beige and navy striped—never flowers. Another friend chose to sit in his wife's chair at the table when children and grandchildren came to join him for dinner. He said, "This way, I can see our family like she saw them. It gives me comfort and helps me feel close to her." Still another purchased a mini-recreational vehicle and traveled around the county visiting national parks and friends along the way. An adult child told his bereavement group friends that after his mother died, he began practicing self-compassion in similar ways she had while grieving the death of her husband, his father. He purchased bouquets of flowers from the grocery store and placed them in the vase his mother had always used.

I hope you will add to the list and share ideas with me. One way to begin practicing self-compassion is to listen to your heart. When you hear it saying, "I'd like to do that," say, "OK!"

WHAT WOULD IT TAKE?

Practices of self-compassion, whether they are religious or not, help us name the cost of our love, the price we pay for it now that our loved one has died. "The pain of grief is just as much part of life as the joy of love," writes Dr. Colin Murray Parkes in *Bereavement: Studies of Grief in Adult Life*. "It is perhaps the price we pay for love, the cost of commitment."

Self-compassion comes in as many forms as there are selves in this world. The spiritual practice for this chapter gets us out in nature. As we learned in an earlier chapter, being present to the moment through our five senses can help us in our grief.

Yesterday Trey, my grandson, and I spent from midmorning until half past sunset outdoors. We alternated between games of HORSE and games of baseball. The morning's rain shower made the green carpet feel especially soft on our bare feet. In the seventh inning stretch, we heard birdsong, watched airline contrails evaporate, and smelled our neighbor's barbecue dinner. Before we went inside, a waxing crescent moon caught our attention, and we stood silently, awed in holy gazing. Simply being outside was healing.

What would it take for you to be kind to yourself? And what might spending time in nature do to the shape and weight of your grief? Frankly, it doesn't matter if you practice self-compassion by walking, gardening, sitting on a park bench, or playing duplicate bridge (my favorite form!). What matters is that, from this time forward, you practice the Platinum Rule. Love yourself as God loves you. When you find it difficult to find a measure of love for yourself, let it serve as a reminder that God's love is limitless. Allow the love for the person you are grieving to transform into self-compassion. Allow that love to fill you so that any compassion you extend to others comes from the abundance of your heart.

SPIRITUAL PRACTICE

NATURE WALK OR SIT

Nature, from the Latin *natura*, means birth. Choosing to heighten awareness of our senses in nature gives birth to new perspectives. These new perspectives can give us hints of what journalist Yasmina Abou-Hilal calls "new ways of coping with our daily tasks, feelings, and emotions." Watch the changing colors of a sunrise or sunset or listen to birdsong. Hold a sprig of honeysuckle, pull out one of the small stems inside the bloom, and taste the sweet drop of nectar that comes out on the tip of the stem. Nature "has magical effects on our minds, bodies and spirits"; in other words, being in nature is a form of self-compassion. Plan to stroll in your neighborhood or sit on a comfortable bench in a nearby park. If you are not able to go outdoors, sit comfortably by a window and gaze.

- Prepare your heart, soul, and mind with a breath prayer.

  Inhale: *Creator of all that is*
  Exhale: *Guide me, open me to wonder*

- Begin your stroll expecting to be delighted. Continue with rapt attention to ordinary features of nature. Simply pay attention.

- Select something in the natural world around you that captures your attention. Is it a leaf? A hawk? A hibiscus blossom? A ladybug? Or better yet, allow it to select *you*. Keep your attention on the natural object by observing it from different angles.

- Engage the imagination of your faith by asking the feature two or three questions below or questions of your own. Allow the feature to ask you the same ones or different ones.

Who do you wish would notice you?
What do you like most about yourself?
What time of the day do you enjoy the most?
How does your appearance change in each season?
What is your favorite season?
What bit of wisdom do you want to share with me?
When was the last time someone noticed and paid attention to you?
What would you like me to pray for you?

- After your stroll, reflect and write about your experience in nature. Write a specific date that you will engage in this spiritual practice again.

CHAPTER 7

HOW CAN WE GO THROUGH GRIEF TOGETHER? AVOIDING NUMBNESS

What separates us from the animals, what separates us from the chaos, is our ability to mourn people we've never met.

—David Levithan

Marla received word from the nurses that her husband, Louis, was near death from COVID-19. She and her children raced to the hospital, where they watched through a window as Louis took his last breath. Even so, in the disbelief that often marks the early days of bereavement, Marla kept thinking, "Maybe it was not really him."

The hospital staff were not able to dress Louis for burial. They were only able to cover him with the blanket that Marla had brought from home. The New Jersey family could not gather in person, so they sat shiva online. Marla's heart was torn farther apart as she watched her parents, on a computer screen in Florida, grieve the death of their son-in-law, whom they loved like a son. "It was unbelievable that they could not be present with me and my children," Marla said. "But it wasn't safe."

During the pandemic another woman, a widowed octogenarian, drove her adult son, an only child, to a hospital when his coronavirus symptoms became worse. Unable to go inside with him, she parked under the hospital's portico and watched him feebly struggle to get inside the emergency room. All the while, she wondered if she would ever see him, talk to him, or hug him again.

"I am just so $@#★&%! angry!" said Jack, the son of a woman who died of the coronavirus. "Angry at the inability to be with her when she needed me, angry at my siblings who weren't there and who didn't seem to care like I did, angry that no one but me seems to get how valuable she was to this world!" Almost a year after his mother's death, Jack's grief-filled anger still weighed heavily on him, impairing his ability and desire to deal with daily life.

The pandemic changed the anatomy of grief, bereavement, and mourning. Grief is all-encompassing, and yet the pandemic required us to isolate ourselves from the very social interaction and spiritual rituals that bring us support and comfort. For those whose loved ones died during the pandemic, the friends and family who would normally pull together when death is imminent were, out of necessity, kept away. Spiritual rituals after death— such as sitting shiva, holding funerals, memorializing our loved ones, or worshiping in community—were eliminated, postponed, or reconfigured with the assistance of technology. We were detached not only by death from a loved one but also from the comfort of family and friends and the consolation of rituals that mark out life and death.

Even those of us who didn't lose a loved one to the coronavirus reported waves of grief that threatened to knock us down. Two-thirds of the respondents to an online survey in 2021 described the pandemic as a grief that diminished their ability to parent, be with those they love, and/or do their jobs well. New and unexpected griefs accumulated as well, as parents worried about the mental health and academic well-being of children learning remotely and as large and small gatherings—birthday and retirement parties, weddings, and events for secular and sacred organizations—had to be canceled, rescheduled, and in many cases canceled again. Levels of despondency and anxiety rose as people realized there was no clear end to new protocols or mandates.

Those of us whose loved ones died *before* the pandemic found ourselves affected as well; cut off from many of the supports we previously had, we found ourselves adrift, unmoored, and lonely. Robert Neimeyer, director of the Portland Institute for Loss and Transition, described mourners of COVID-19 deaths as having a "sticky, heavy grief that doesn't yield to the passage of time."

Sticky, heavy grief: that description is apt. The pandemic interrupted our ability to grieve with others. Any grief experienced all alone becomes a weight, and it is hard to move underneath it. Coming together with others who are grieving doesn't bring our loved one back, but it helps us metabolize the horror and sadness.

How does isolation shape our grief? What are the rituals and supports we can offer to each other in times of grief? And how can we connect with trusted others in ways that help us carry the sticky heaviness of grief?

GLOBAL ALERT, COMMUNAL GRIEF

The millions of people who die from a global cataclysm or national catastrophe—a virus, a war, an earthquake, a forest fire—can overwhelm and numb us. If the numbers are beyond comprehension, the names are entirely out of reach as well. We struggle to imagine the countless family and friends who grieved their deaths—and still are. The deceased millions possessed immeasurable skills and talents that blessed our world and are now gone.

An event like a pandemic or natural disaster or war is both too massive for our brains to comprehend and too horrific for us to turn away. During the global pandemic, our losses were too immense to quantify and too intimate to ignore.

When physical symptoms of COVID-19 begin and intensify, emotional responses of the patient and family do likewise. When a diagnosis is confirmed, everyone enters a heightened state of alert. And the inability to be near a loved one fighting COVID-19 at home is agonizing. Not being able to be with a loved one who is hospitalized—gasping for air, struggling with fever and chills, or holding on to dear life by breathing only on a ventilator—is tortuous.

We want to be present with our loved one in distress to speak words of love and encouragement, to hold a hand or wipe a brow, to advocate for them, and to offer verbal and silent prayers. Being kept away from our loved ones during a public health crisis stands in direct opposition to our natural instincts.

The isolation brought about by lockdowns confounded and complicated this grief and anxiety. We know that the effects of the pandemic on our physical health and the effects of social isolation on our mental health were massive. Psychologist Julianne Holt-Lunstand wrote, "Given that humans are a social species, this is our biology signaling a need to reconnect socially, just like hunger signals us to eat, and thirst signals us to drink water. Proximity to others, particularly trusted others, signals safety. When we lack proximity to trusted others our brain and body may respond with a state of heightened alert."

There is healing power in companionship or comradeship or camaraderie. When our communities unite in healing, it helps the healing process for everyone. "Communal grieving offers something that we cannot get when we grieve by ourselves," writes Burkinabe writer and activist Sobonfu Somé. "Through acknowledgment, validation, and witnessing, communal grieving allows us to experience a level of healing that is deeply and profoundly freeing."

The pandemic was one form of communal grief event; here we will look at just two more. While we don't have time to look at all the ways that grief can rip through entire communities, we can see some common strands.

MASS SHOOTINGS

Communal and national grief is far-reaching—rolling across the mountains, prairies, deserts, and winding its way into our psyches. With each mass shooting, grief ravages our communities. The cumulative effect of such grief leaves our communities traumatized and forever changed. By May 24, 2022, there had already been 212 mass shootings in the United States during that calendar year (twenty-seven of them in schools). According to the Gun Violence Archive, the United States ended 2021 with 693 mass shootings; 2020 with 611; and 2019 with 417.

Grief's immediate and numbing shock didn't ease the horror of hearing about yet one more mass shooting, this one in Uvalde, Texas, leaving nineteen children and two teachers dead. The morning after the Uvalde shooting, after tossing and turning in bed and listening to an overnight downpour, I decided to go for a walk. Dove-gray clouds filled the skies. There was a chill in the morning air that seemed to match the temperature of my blood. I walk and prayed, walked and prayed. I noticed that the neighborhood warblers were silent. Breezes shook raindrops from the trees on top of my head. The forlorn color of the day, the songless birds, the tears of trees: it seemed that all creation was in grief. I felt a small measure of comfort in being in sync with creation.

The walk turned pieces of my sadness into renewed conviction to action: to be an instrument of change and compassion. When we experience grief on a national scale like a mass shooting, we may find fury and sadness turned to activism and commitment to be part of the solution.

DEATH BY SUICIDE

One morning in ministry, I received a call that a young man had died by suicide. I made my way to the family's home, and as I pulled into the driveway, I saw other parents walking their children to school and walking their dogs. On the family' porch, on both sides of the door, were two terracotta pots of red geraniums. Ringing the doorbell, I thought that everything looked so beautiful and normal that I almost wondered if this news was real.

But when the young man's father opened the door, desolation personified stood before me. Without saying a word, he led me to the kitchen where his wife, dressed in a housecoat, was letting the sink hold her up while she was staring blankly out the window. Everything was quiet. It was as if sorrow's curtains of silence draped from ceiling to floor.

After a death by suicide, family and friends are floored with disbelief and consumed with questions. We tend to believe that if we knew the why, we would be better able to reconcile our grief. We are haunted for years by litanies of "what if we had . . ." scenarios, hoping for insights to our excruciating pain.

High school classmates of Grant Halliburton voted him Most Likely to Become a Recording Artist and featured him in the senior yearbook as Coolest Kid on Campus. In 2005, at age 19, Grant died by suicide. Members of his family decided to change the litany of questions to a litany of possibilities. They asked, *"What if we do* form a network of mental health resources for children, teens, and young adults; promote better mental health; and prevent suicide?"* In 2006, months after Grant's death, his mom, Vanita; his dad, Alan; and one of his sister's, Amy, established the Grant Halliburton Foundation to answer their questions, ask other questions, and provide resources to youth and their families. Today, Vanita and Amy help families and young people recognize the signs of mental illness through a variety of avenues including mental health education, collaboration, encouragement, and information.

After the suicide of his father, author and editor Albert Y. Hsu said, "What has been helpful to me is the realization that my father did not kill himself to abandon me. He did what he did to end his pain, not to cause pain for me." This truth has set him free to study ongoing research, write, and speak to survivors of suicide to bring measures of comfort through his experience and wisdom. Another invaluable resource is the American Foundation for Suicide Prevention (AFSP). Local chapters across the country host conferences and activities to raise awareness for the resources available to families and the larger communities.

DETACHED FROM RITUAL

The pandemic led us to reappraise the previously taken-for-granted informal and formal rituals surrounding the death of a loved one. We may not have been aware of the intrinsic value of shared grief that comes from these rituals.

We had little conception of the magnitude of comfort provided when friends and colleagues simply appear at the door with no other motive than to share in the present sorrow. The acts of embracing in silence, wiping away tears, sharing stories or anecdotes, and bringing food for body and soul soften the pain of grief.

Journalist Karan Johnson writes that according to scientists, these informal and formal practices "convince our brains of constancy and predictability as ritual buffers against uncertainty and anxiety." When our brains didn't have those buffers, they sometimes went haywire.

The inability to hold formal rituals of faith left survivors anxious and angry as they decided what to do. Just as she had feared, the octogenarian we met at the beginning of the chapter did not get to talk to or hug her son again. Instead, she stood by his grave for a brief ceremony, standing six feet from the minister and six feet from the funeral home director. The three of them were the only people present at her son's COVID-era funeral.

After her husband died, Tena found herself in raw, visceral grief—and also in a quandary about what to do for a memorial service. Family and friends lived as far as east (Florida) is from the west (Washington). Her pastor suggested that she consider having a memorial service via videoconference. At first the idea seemed bizarre, but it soon appeared to be the best option. More than one hundred people gathered in little squares on her computer screen. Tena was grateful that her husband's mother could see the outpouring of love, hear the stories about her larger-than-life son, listen to scripture's promises, and pray in unison with others, though distanced from them by thousands of miles.

Some families chose to delay funeral plans until COVID-19 went away, only to face waves of variants that resulted in rolling lockdowns. Delay after delay, decision after decision weighed heavily on the hearts of the living.

Sometimes, thankfully, grace did appear. One family member who attended a memorial service months after the death reflected, "I believe I got more out of the memorial service since it was held months after my father's death. Immediately after his death, I was completely distraught. I don't think I would have remembered a single thing. Having it later, I could take in the prayers and beautiful music. It was healing. Maybe we ought to always wait."

Many of us learned more about different ways of grieving as we watched so many neighbors and friends and family members around us go through it. We learned that some people are *instrumental grievers*. These individuals tend to think their way through grief, like problem solving. Their comfort in grief comes from doing activities and taking care of the necessary tasks associated with illness and death. Instrumental grievers are usually the ones who ask questions of funeral directors and speak for the family at memorial services.

Other people are *intuitive grievers*. They openly express their feelings, which ebb and flow in raw and lingering grief. They are viewed as being "more emotional" than others because they are comfortable expressing, sharing, and talking about their feelings. Many people used to view these styles of grief as gender-based. Stereotypically, men were understood as instrumental grievers, while women were considered intuitive grievers. Today we are learning to accept that people of all genders demonstrate a variety of responses to grief, ones that are not easily predictable or linked to gender identity.

One intuitive griever named Sabila Khan found that, during the pandemic, she needed a space larger than her home to process the death of her father, Shafqat Khan. She was yearning for conversation with others who had experienced the death of relatives and friends from COVID-19. She founded a Facebook group called Covid-19 Loss Support for Family & Friends. Through this venue, she could give voice to her feelings and have them affirmed, and she could support others too.

Still, she says, "the fact that [my father] was alone and aware and probably knew that he would never see us again—it's just something that will haunt me for the rest of my life." One participant of the Facebook group wrote, "It was a life-saver for me. You can go on at three in the morning and post, 'I can't sleep,' and you will have 30 COVID-bereaved people respond."

When we are in grief, our hearts are consumed with pain. This heart pain intensifies with every beat, pumping bloody chills through our veins. When we are in pain, we often long to be numb. When we are numb, we often wish we could feel something. Both when we are numb and when we aren't, we are hyperaware that life will never be the same, and we have no idea what comes next.

RITUALS

Prayer services and other rituals that mark and honor grief can help us pierce through the numbness. Rituals provide refuge and strength. Amid the internal and external chaos of grief, rituals provide a familiar order. Such order places no expectations or demands on us other than our presence. In the bewildering fear of an unknown future, rituals remind us of promises of old. Often these promises come in the form of sacred stories, where those who went before us overcame fear with courage, curiosity, and trust in God. When we are grief-stricken, we often want to disengage with time. But we can find refuge in the patterns and rhythms and spaces between the beginning, middle, and end of rituals.

Rituals give us the emotional strength we need to carry our sorrows. Although we can practice rituals alone, the majority are practiced communally, with those who love us and want the best for us. In community, we literally see and hear that we are not alone in our grief.

My friends Shahnaz and Hamid experienced the unspeakable death of their only child, Nina. Although there is no widespread, formal ritual in Islam for marking the anniversary of a loved one's death, in Iran, where Shahnaz and Hamid are from, such a ritual exists. The family of the loved one goes to the graveyard to pray, and then they prepare the loved one's favorite dishes and eat together. A year after Nina's death, Shahnaz and Hamid practiced self-compassion by engaging in a form of this ritual. They purchased a bench to place by Nina's grave. It was crafted with two hearts on each side, representing their love.

Shahnaz and Hamid designed a ritual and asked friends who had loved Nina and shared their grief to lead it. We gathered at Nina's grave. A Canadian friend read a poem by Hafiz, a Persian poet. I read the beatitudes, a list of blessings from Jesus's Sermon on the Mount. A Jewish friend, the father of Nina's best friend from school, gave each of us a butterfly to release into the canopy of blue sky above us. United by our love for Nina, Shahnaz, and Hamid, we turned our gazes upward, as dazzling sunlight seemed to touch each monarch's wing. We wept together at this cruel reversal that had required parents to bury a child. We embraced one another. And we accepted Shahnaz and Hamid's invitation to Nina's favorite restaurant for a meal of kabab koobideh (Iranian meat kabab) and two of her favorite stews: fesenjān (chicken and pomegranate) and ghormeh sabzi (lamb and kidney beans).

Sometimes the sequence of life events occurs at such rapid speed that years fly by before we confront our deepest, most painful grief. Jennifer shared with me that she had experienced a miscarriage fourteen years earlier. At a routine OB-GYN visit, as she and her husband, Paul, were gazing through a sonogram at the baby they called Sweet Pea, the doctor informed them that the baby's heart was no longer beating.

For the next fourteen years, Jennifer had focused her time on both her corporate career and on nurturing and supporting those around her. After four years of fighting infertility, she and Paul adopted a son and daughter, moved across the country, and engaged in community activities. This schedule provided no extra time and drained any energy Jennifer may have had for addressing unreconciled grief from both the pregnancy loss and inability to get pregnant.

Now, more than a dozen years later, the memories of this child loss were still vivid and present. Jennifer could still feel the ecstasy of pregnancy, and she could feel the utter despondency of Sweet Pea's death.

But Jennifer had hidden her grief behind an "I'm Fine" mask for so long that she both longed to take the mask off and was afraid to do so. She had worn it so long she did not know who she would be without it. On multiple occasions, Jennifer had single-handedly attempted to move through the grief, but it remained stuck. She recognized that she needed the hands of a trustworthy and experienced grief therapist. Regular sessions became her form of self-compassion. In each session's homework, tears surfaced that watered sadness and anger, high expectations and shame, and denial and fear. Eventually, Jennifer found, the mask was pliable enough for removal. She was ready to carry her sorrow rather than run away from it.

To mark such transformation, and as a kindness to themselves, Jennifer and Paul asked me to lead them in a ritual that would recognize Sweet Pea's steadfast influence on their lives, as well as their desire to release threadbare patterns of thought and action. We walked a labyrinth, an ancient formation designed for prayer and meditation that contains no dead ends and consists of a single path toward the center. (If you want to walk a labyrinth, search online for ones in your area. You can also experience praying through a labyrinth on a smaller scale by tracing your finger slowly over the design of a labyrinth and praying as you do so. See the resource section for the drawing of a labyrinth and instructions.)

Once we reached the center of the labyrinth, Jennifer and Paul and I sat in the center of God's love. We listened to scripture, silence, and prayers, and we released former things on water-soluble paper, placing the pages in water and remembering our baptism. Jennifer and Paul read lines from a litany for release to each other. (You can find that litany at the end of the book.)

I pronounced God's blessing on Jennifer and Paul. We left the center of the labyrinth and walked the pathway back toward the opening. In the silence, we called to heart, soul, and mind our acceptance of God's gifts.

SUPPORTS

Natural disasters like the global pandemic, mass killings, deaths by suicide, and human-made destruction like war and climate change beckon many of us to take a personal spiritual inventory. The great number of deaths from events like these prompt reflections and conversations on theodicy (why does God permit evil and suffering?), the value of community, and the meaning of life in a world where pandemics kill millions, where children of God are murdered, and where forms of violence attempt to reign. Many people have lost hope for better tomorrows.

No one close to me died of COVID; however, midway through 2020, I began feeling emotionally flat. As I allowed myself to feel the fullness of flatness, it dawned on me that I had felt the same way while caring for Bob, my husband, during his journey with Alzheimer's. My grief was resurfacing.

Walking with Bob in his final years had been a lonely journey, and the loneliness of pandemic lockdowns took me back to those days. I entertained friends and family in our home less frequently in that era because of Bob's limitations; some friends were uneasy being around him since he was nonverbal and no longer the inquisitive and quick-witted friend and mentor they had known. That memory of intense isolation echoed inside me now, as I spent so much time alone. Spun into a downward spiral of grief two years after Bob's death, I missed him more, which I hadn't known was possible. At the same time, I was grateful that he wasn't having to live through the distress of a global pandemic.

A global health emergency like the pandemic can interrupt and resurface previous griefs. Many of us became aware that we needed help. We could not do the work of grieving the compounded losses of a global pandemic on our own. As I realized that my deep grief over my husband's death had resurfaced in a new way, I heard my inner coach instruct me to connect with a spiritual community for support.

So I registered for several online prayer workshops. One facilitator, aware that COVID-19 had given many of us an out-of-body sense of being or a feeling like floating in space, had us place our hands over our hearts to center our thoughts to the steadiness of our heartbeats. We kept that posture throughout the class.

We gave voice to prayers for our COVID-afflicted world. We prayed for the millions grieving, for the physical and mental health of frontline responders, and for those who had lost employment and financial resources. We prayed for world leaders and for peace amid political differences driving wedges between families and friends. We prayed for the more than 100,000 children who had lost a parent or caregiver.

Love for relatives and friends who have died has often been the motivation for those who remain to establish foundations, nonprofits, and programs in their memory. These causes have visions and missions with far-reaching effects to serve, inspire, and support those wrestling with grief.

LAMENT

The sacred time and space of prayer workshops renewed my understanding of the need for relying on spiritual resources in times of distress. I was reminded that prayer changes many things, but most importantly it changes us. The change for me came in turning away from solitary self-pity toward the age-old communal prayer of lament.

Henri Nouwen taught me new insights about the relationship between lament and care. Care "finds its roots in the Gothic *Kara,* which means lament," Nouwen writes. The "basic meaning of care is 'to grieve, to experience sorrow, to cry out with.'" Genuine care, therefore, does not begin by giving tangible resources or by using power and influence to open doors for persons in need. Rather, genuine care begins by *being with* being at one with all who grieve, sorrow, and cry out. Lament is care. Care is lament, and this act of grieving is done *with* others. There are strong traditions of communal lament in most religious traditions around the world.

A blessing in my life is the friendship I share with Margie. Margie is always up for a Friday night dice game of Farkle, more than willing to help me bake gluten-free communion bread, and picks me up in her red convertible VW Bug for the Purim festival at her synagogue. That blessing was doubled when I became acquainted with her mom, Sonya, whom everyone knew as Sunny. Sunny was the grand dame of her circles, and her arms opened wide enough to welcome any- and everyone into her community.

Days after Sunny's death at age ninety-five, Margie invited me to attend a Shiva Minyan at Congregation Shearith Israel. The prayer-filled service included time for the rabbi and persons of all ages to share stories of Sunny's influence on their lives. During the service, the Mourner's Kaddish was recited. The prayer focuses solely on God, Creator of heaven and earth, who is affected by this death. The image of God on Sunny's face no longer lives in the world, causing the image of God to be decreased in the world. In recognition of her death and in memory of her, worshippers say to God *yitgadal*, "May you be increased." (You'll find a version of the Kaddish in the resources section.)

Sitting shiva is a Jewish ritual of lament that focuses on the mourner. Following tradition, Margie left her house door open after her mother's death so that a knock or ring of the doorbell would not startle or distract her from her sorrow. Visitors would walk in and place dishes of food on the dining table. We sat by Margie and showed our love by allowing her to initiate conversation about her mother. She shared memories, some of which made us laugh— including the time that Sunny, much to her daughter's chagrin, wore the same outfit to synagogue on both days of Rosh Hashanah. As we sat together, Margie let us know Sunny believed that walking cured all life's troubles and woes. Between stories, we kept silent and respected her and our own tears. It was a reminder that any length life is too short for all the love we long to give and receive and that the life of a loved one is far greater than the sum of the stories that can be shared about them.

Some people choose to participate in rituals of lament from their own religious tradition. Some find meaning in practices from another tradition or in designing one of their own, with the help of friends or family. This chapter's spiritual practice is writing a lament for yourself, a community to which you belong, or our world. Many find this practice of writing out a prayer of lament initially uncomfortable, even scary. Shaking a fist in raw and honest anger and bitterness to God can feel unnerving. Scriptures from many faith traditions, however, testify that God not only hears our anger and despondency but also has the compassionate capacity to receive it. In my tradition, Christianity, I can think of numerous laments that God received from righteous people, including Hannah, David, Job, Isaiah—and Jesus himself.

In times of individual and communal grief, we discover many truths about our capacity to love and grieve, to respect and judge, and to be generous and cautious. We find that we can be both compassionate and indifferent, and we learn to pray and pray and pray some more. We discover new gifts and opportunities to serve those who are grieving, and we acknowledge grief's pervasive presence and its many, many layers.

SPIRITUAL PRACTICE

PRAYER OF LAMENT

Prayers of lament emerge from the gap between our *worldview*, or expectation (how we believe the world can be), and the present *circumstance* (the reality). Laments give words to our unreconciling struggles:

- believing that air quality is relatively satisfactory—and yet invisible, potentially deadly particles of viruses are swimming in the air waiting to be inhaled;

- believing that communities and highways are safe— and yet each day people are killed through violence, systemic injustice, and vehicle crashes;

- believing that if we practice healthy habits of exercise, nutrition, and sleep, we will live a long life—and yet any number of diseases indiscriminately invade our bodies and bring destruction.

In the 150 biblical songs found in the book of Psalms, there are fifty-eight laments. Forty-two are psalms of individual lament, and sixteen are written on behalf of a community or nation. Each lament appeals to God for mercy and assumes a measure of confidence of God's character and God's intimate interest in our welfare. Take a look at the psalms or find a passage of scripture from your own tradition that speaks to the pain of loss and the comfort of God.

Writing your own prayer of lament can allow you to put into words all the feelings that you have about your loved one's death or about a national or global crisis in which many lives are lost. It can help you stay attuned to the feelings of loss and fear and anger rather than become numb to them.

- **Prepare:** Get ready to write your own lament by centering your heart and mind with the following breath prayer or one of your own.

  Inhale: *God of truth and grace,*
  Exhale: *Encourage me to be honest.*

- **Turn to God:** Read Psalm 77:1–3 several times. Then, in your journal or on a piece of paper, write your own *turning toward the Divine*.

  > I cry aloud to God, aloud to God, that God may hear me.
  > In the day of my trouble I seek the Lord;
  > in the night my hand is stretched out without wearying; my soul refuses to be comforted.
  > I think of God, and I moan; I meditate, and my spirit faints.

- **Complain to God:** Read Psalm 13:1–2 and then write your *complaint*.

  > How long, O LORD? Will you forget me forever?
  > How long will you hide your face from me?
  > How long must I bear pain in my soul and have sorrow in my heart all day long?
  > How long shall my enemy be exalted over me?

- **Ask God for what you want:** Read Psalm 13:4a and write your *request*.

  > Consider and answer me, O LORD my God
  > Give light to my eyes, or I will sleep the sleep of death.

- **Write an affirmation of trust:** Read Psalm 13:5 and write your own *sense of trust*.

But I trusted in your steadfast love; my heart shall rejoice in your salvation. I will sing to the LORD, because the LORD has dealt bountifully with me.

- Write an abbreviated version of your version in the provided illustration. Fill in your worldview (your *expectation*) on the left hand. Write the specifics of your circumstance (your *reality*) on the right hand. Summarize your lament in the gap between the hands.

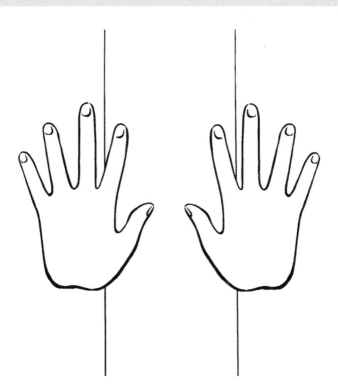

CHAPTER 8

WHAT DO WE DO ABOUT FORGIVENESS? REFRAMING RECONCILIATION

I learned a long time ago that some people would rather die than forgive.

It's a strange truth, but forgiveness is a painful and difficult process.

It's not something that happens overnight.

It's an evolution of the heart.

—**Sue Monk Kidd**

Drummers and bagpipers in tartan kilts, sporrans, and ghillie brogues led the recessional of clergy and worshipers to the courtyard for Scottish games and haggis. It was Reformation Sunday, on which we remembered Martin Luther's posting of the Ninety-Five Theses in Wittenberg, Germany, as well as the Scotch immigrants who brought Presbyterianism to America.

Not having the stomach for haggis, I made my way back to the sanctuary to gather my belongings. The skirl of "Amazing Grace" on the bagpipes filtered through the walls and windows. I sang along, giving thanks that God is full of grace and mercy.

When I got to the line "was blind, but now I see," I spotted a woman sitting alone on a back pew. Making my way to greet her, I noticed that her cheeks were covered in tears. Rays of sun streamed through the windows, and in that light, I thought her face looked like that of an angel.

"I'm home!" she said. "Years ago, I moved to the States from Scotland, and today I feel like I'm back home." The woman proceeded to tell me more about her life. Senga lived alone and had stage IV cancer. She desperately wanted to become involved in a church community. Our friendship immediately took root that day, and over the years, it grew.

When Senga died, my heart filled with sadness. When I met her children to plan a memorial service, though, my sadness shattered into shards of bewilderment.

"I hated my mother," Senga's daughter announced. Nothing like cutting to the chase, I thought, taken aback.

Her son jumped in. "You know our mother's name wasn't Senga, right?" By this point, the only thing I knew was that planning this memorial service was going to be a challenge.

"Her name was Agnes, but she never liked that name," her son continued. "So being a precocious child, she reversed the letters in Agnes and came up with Senga. The name stuck."

Senga's adult children shared other facts about their family life. There were times of unemployment, multiple moves, divorce, saying one thing and acting differently, meaning one thing and saying another. Vitriol and sadness permeated the room. At one point Senga's daughter stood up; said, "I'm not coming to the funeral"; and walked out of my office.

A heavy silence bore down on those of us who remained. My heart ached for everyone involved—even for Senga, who was dead. Words from author Patricia Ennis drifted across my mind: "The choice to withhold forgiveness slowly but effectively destroys family unity."

The choice to withhold forgiveness is fraught with complexities. A cohort of pastors and spiritual directors whom I meet with regularly often discusses the simultaneous need for and difficulty of forgiveness. Forgiveness is messy, we say. There's so much pain to sift through. We forget that it's a process. We tend to rush to forgiveness and don't spend appropriate time on the hurt, restorative justice, and healing involved. Sometimes we *like* feeling angry and resentful toward a person or system. And sometimes we need to forgive ourselves.

When death occurs, grief can be complicated by lack of forgiveness for actions large and small. There's nothing easy about forgiveness when both parties are living. Is there a way to reframe what reconciliation means when one person has died and the one remains? When a loved one dies before we've been able to either ask for or extend forgiveness, what do we do?

First off, it's important to name your anger. This is difficult because, as we learned earlier, anger is a secondary emotion that likes to cover up other emotions, especially sadness and fear. It often takes time to peel the layers of anger away to get to the heart of the issue. Litsa Williams, coauthor of *What's Your Grief?*, wrote a blog post that includes a comprehensive list of possibilities where forgiveness would be a gift. Interestingly, she started out with the anger we may feel toward a loved one who has died. Here's a portion:

- An old, unresolved hurt that you never reconciled before their death.
- A death by suicide, in which you feel anger that a loved one intentionally ended their life.
- A death by overdose, drunk driving, etc., in which you feel anger that they used a substance and put themselves in harm's way.
- A death by risky behavior (high-speed driving, risky sports, riding a motorcycle, etc.) in which the death feels avoidable.
- Anger that someone didn't "fight" hard enough, common if someone opted to stop treatment, or not seek treatment, for an illness.
- Anger that someone didn't take care of themselves, common if a death was due to heart disease, diabetes, lung cancer, or some other disease in which you feel

a different lifestyle choice could have prevented the disease or outcome. This could include anger about a late diagnosis because someone didn't go to the doctor.

- Anger about things that a person said or did while they were ill. This could also take the form of anger about things they didn't say or didn't do.

There is also such difficulty in forgiving oneself. Yet like compassion and the Platinum Rule mentioned earlier, it is important for us to accept the divine forgiveness available to us so that we can have a fuller understanding of its restorative power.

THE SPIRITUALITY OF FORGIVENESS

The Abrahamic faith traditions—Judaism, Christianity, and Islam—share a family unity regarding God's forgiving nature and God's desire for us to extend and receive forgiveness from others. In the Jewish faith, Yom Kippur is set apart as the Day of Atonement. On this day, members practice Teshuva, which defined means "returning." The act of Teshuva requires an individual to end, regret, confess, and repent of a harmful act. When a person who has caused harm apologizes, the wronged person is religiously bound to forgive. Even without an apology, however, forgiveness is a holy act, according to the book of Deuteronomy.

The central tenet in the Christian faith is forgiveness. The focus is on Jesus, God incarnate, who was and is wronged yet graciously initiates the act of forgiveness through his death on the cross. Before drawing his last breath, Jesus said, "Father, forgive them" (Luke 23:34). God's love-filled power resurrected Jesus from death to show the world, for all time, God's victory over death and sin and to reveal the promise of new life. As the late Bishop Desmond Tutu said, "Forgiveness is nothing less than the way we heal the world."

Forgiveness is a critical aspect of Islam as well. When Muslims ask for forgiveness with repentance, they trust that Allah, All Merciful and Forgiving, will forgive their sin. Yet before Allah grants forgiveness, Allah requests that the repenter vow that they will not commit that sin again. Allah's forgiveness is a prerequisite for peace. The word *Islam* is derived from a Semitic word *salem*, which means "peace."

The pain of bereavement is often multiplied by a need to give or receive forgiveness. Less than ideal family dynamics and clashing personalities tend to surface in the wake of a loved one's death—and in neon colors, I might add. During my years in ministry, I encountered many people carrying long-held resentments against the living and the dead. Senga's family was hardly alone in their resentment-filled grief.

Years ago, I was introduced to another Agnes: Agnes Sanford, author and founder of the Inner Healing movement. A friend gave me a set of Sanford's cassette tapes on the topic of forgiveness. Sanford's ministry focused on guiding individuals to recall painful memories and, through a process, forgive the one who had harmed them. One interview that Sanford held with a young child who had been harmed by an adult reveals that forgiveness and healing are only possible when a person has a thoughtful and sincere desire to engage in the process. The story went something like this:

Sanford asked, "Do you want to forgive this person?"

"No," said the child.

"Do you *want* to want to forgive this person?" Sanford asked.

"No. I don't *want* to want to forgive this person," responded the child.

"Well, do you *want to want* to want to forgive this person?" continued Sanford.

"Maybe one eyelash length," said the child.

So if you want to want to *want* to forgive a person, it just might be sufficient. In this chapter we will practice a model for forgiveness. It's important to note here that families and friends who experience conflict after a loved one dies need time to grieve even as they work to experience measures of healing and reconciliation with each other. There's nothing easy about giving and receiving forgiveness, especially during times of bereavement. And yet there is nothing so beautiful as the countenance of those who have reconciled with loved ones, living or deceased, or who have experienced the grace of self-forgiveness.

EXAMINING OURSELVES

During the time of bereavement, long after raw grief has subsided, we often withdraw into a cocoon of introspection. We ponder our mortality. We ponder how we desire to live out the unknown remainder of our days after we struggle for release from this cocoon of bereavement. We ponder the importance of our relationships with family members and with those forged by the deepest bonds of friendship.

Attention to these ponderings may beckon us to seek reconciliation with a person or persons. More often than not, in my own life I have felt inadequate to reach reconciliation. After all, I realize I have done wrong, and I want forgiveness. For insight, I read books and blogs and sought professional counseling. Repeatedly I'd read or hear that a motivation for seeking someone else's forgiveness is that it will make *me* feel better.

Seeking forgiveness so that *we* may feel better seems, to me, to be the wrong motive—like it's off-base or hollow. I return to the theological understanding of the imago dei to search for a true and sincere motive. This theological doctrine in Judaism, Christianity, and some Sufi sects of Islam declares that humankind is created in the image and likeness (not exactness) of God. The compelling motive for seeking another's forgiveness is that we have committed a double sin. We have offended God and a person created in God's image. The first step in the process of forgiveness is to do an honest and thorough self-examination. It's a step that takes time and commitment.

If you feel unsure where to begin in self-examination, try naming a trait or behavior that you dislike in other people. My great-grandmother used to say, "The faults that you see in others are most likely your own. That's why you notice them." Chances are that one, or a combination, of the seven deadly sins may come to mind: pride, gluttony, lust, sloth, greed, envy, and licentiousness.

Awareness of oneself can be embarrassing and shameful. Examining yourself can also be freeing if you believe (even one eyelash length!) that you are loved and fully known by our Creator. Rest assured that God is already aware of everything you admit. In the sacred company of the Divine, you will be able to accept the divine gift of forgiveness for yourself. God yearns for you to accept this gift of love. It's impossible to surprise God by your sins—or by your gifts, which are needed in this world.

"There is so much good in the worst of us, and so much bad in the best of us, that it behooves us all not to judge the rest of us": this quotation has been attributed to many different people—Edward Wallis Hoch, James Truslow Adams, and Robert Louis Stevenson, to name a few. But no matter who said it, its message is singular: self-examination enriches our relationships with God and others. It heightens our awareness of God's grace upon grace extended to each image-bearer. Self-examination enlightens us to not only the worst in ourselves but also the best in others—even those we have hurt and those who have hurt us.

After you have examined yourself, repented, and received forgiveness from God, it's almost time to forgive the person who has mistreated you.

Almost.

ASKING FOR FORGIVENESS

First, though: spend time writing down your request for forgiveness. Writing connects your hands to your heart and helps you clarify your thoughts. Below is a framework that I have found helpful. The **bold** print represents what to do, and the *italics* what not to do.

> **I want and need to talk with you. I hope and trust that you will listen. I did [name action or words], which hurt you.**
>> *Not taking full responsibility.*

> **I regret that my [words, actions, lack of action] caused you pain. I ask for your forgiveness so that we can renew our relationship.**
>> *Not being sincere. Taking lightly your regret and the pain caused and/or being defensive.*

> **Now is the time to wait in silence. If you have an urge to speak before the person speaks, think to yourself: WAIT. This is a reminder to ask yourself: Why Am I Talking? Keep in mind that you have spent much time and preparation for this moment; however, it's the other person's first time to hear and consider your apology.**
>> *Not respecting the silence or the other person's feelings.*

Another person's consideration of your request for forgiveness is out of your control. In church one Sunday morning, my seven-year-old grandson leaned over toward his mother. The day before he had said something to a classmate, Hallie, that he regretted. Now he whispered to his mom, "I told Hallie that I was sorry that I hurt her feelings. She said, 'I don't accept your apology.'"

He paused, incredulous. "Can she even *do* that?"

She *can* do that. So can the person from whom you've requested forgiveness. It may be that the person needs more time. It may be that they want to ask how you plan to change as you move forward. The power of apology lies in "the exchange of shame and power between the offender and the offended," the late psychiatrist Aaron Lazare wrote in a *Psychology Today* article.

In the best scenarios, the offended person extends welcome and gives their time and attention to your request for forgiveness. The offended welcomes the experience of mutual healing. Once the offended offers words of forgiveness, the offender often expresses gratitude. The conversation can then turn to new ways the two parties will interact.

In the worst scenarios, the offended will not take you seriously when you ask for forgiveness. Or they may minimize whatever happened to avoid the conversation. Their inexperience with forgiveness may come across as making light of the situation. You may hear statements such as these: "Oh, it didn't really bother me in the first place." "You didn't mean it." "I think you were just tired or had too much to drink." "That's in the past."

Hear them out, without interruption or rebuttal. When they finish speaking, consider saying, "You are correct. It was in the past. But going forward, I am committed to making our future different. Will you forgive me?"

These steps take practice. And when families find themselves entrenched in conflict after a loved one's death, they can be especially difficult. But we never exhaust life's circumstances nor our need to receive and give forgiveness.

FORGIVENESS AFTER DEATH

But what do we do if the offended, or the offender, has died? If we cannot ask for and receive forgiveness—or have our forgiveness sought? Death seems to have taken away all opportunity for an in-person conversation to reach reconciliation.

Yet if you feel the nudge to forgive or to ask forgiveness from a loved one who has already died, you still can. Even if it's impossible for your loved one to extend forgiveness to you in real time, you can trust that asking for their forgiveness will reach them in some ultimate way. The conversation, spiritual in nature, can take place.

First, we must dismiss an often-heard truism: Forgiveness is giving up all hope for a better past. The focus of reconciliation through forgiveness is future oriented. While death removes the opportunity for in-person conversations around forgiveness, it does not take away the opportunity for love. The death of someone you have offended, or someone who offended you, may bring a new understanding of the depth of love between you. That love keeps the way open for conversations, through prayer, and to a future sense of peace and reconciliation.

When I was young, I had sometimes wished my dad were dead so that neither of us would have to deal with his addiction to alcohol. I stopped wishing that by the time I was an adult. My dad died hours after surgery to remove his left lung. The shock of his death leaves me with no memory of driving home from the hospital and stopping at the grocery store. What I do remember is suddenly becoming aware that I was standing in my house, holding a gallon of milk, and looking at a spectacularly beautiful floral arrangement that had been delivered and placed on my dining room table. In a flash, words given to me by the Holy Spirit rolled out of my heart, "Daddy, I'm so glad I didn't want you to die. And I'm so glad that you didn't die drunk." It's hard to capture this experience in words, but this moment felt like a reconciliation. It felt like I was paving the way to a new and lasting relationship with my dad even though he was now dead.

Life itself is a mystery; why should death be any different? Depending where you're coming from, this next part may sound strange to you; however, I believe our loved ones hear our prayers, and I believe that they can engage in conversation with us through our prayers and dreams. I'm open to the idea that they grant us the insights that we think we garner through conversation or lived experience or literature or nature. I sometimes hope that Senga's daughter is visited by her mother, and that the two of them are somehow given a redemption of their memories and reconciliation.

As a pastor, I have had the grace-filled opportunity to pronounce the assurance of God's forgiveness in worship services. A portion the traditional words say, "The old life has gone; a new life has begun. In Jesus Christ, we are forgiven." The work of forgiveness may seem insurmountable, especially when it seems foreclosed on by death. But if we just take the next step, we can walk toward a reconciliation that surpasses space and time. Step by step in the process, reconciliation can occur, with the living and the dead. It may not always happen in the way we envision, but each step matters.

Rabbi Shawn Zell, a colleague, told me that he counseled someone who could not reach a resolution with a person who was unable to forgive, which made it difficult for them to grieve. After many sessions with this person, Zell heard forgiveness and grief in a new way. If you are in a similar situation, read his poem in the resources section and discover new pathways toward reconciliation.

After the death of a loved one, we can stay connected, or in spiritual relationship, with that person. In Dr. Ira Byock's book *The Four Things That Matter Most: A Book about Living*, he shares the wisdom he learned from hundreds of persons he met through his medical practice and through hospice and palliative care. They taught him "the four things that matter most": "Please forgive me. I forgive you. Thank you. I love you."

The spiritual practice for this chapter, the mandala, can help us frame or reframe reconciliation by giving space and time to focus on the full circle of relationships—forgiveness, thanksgiving, and love. Many people and cultures have vouched for the mandala's intrinsic meaning. Buddhists, and Hindus have all derived meaning from the mandala and its captivating beauty. Psychoanalyst Carl Jung said,

"The mandala is an archetypal image whose occurrence is attested throughout the ages. It signifies the wholeness of the Self. This circular image represents the wholeness of the psychic ground or, to put it in mythic terms, the divinity incarnate."

The mandala (Sanskrit for "circle," or "completion") has a long history, dating back to about eighth-century India. It is recognized for its deep spiritual meaning and the way it represents wholeness. The "circle with a center" pattern is the basic structure of creation that is reflected from the micro to the macro in the world. It is a pattern found in nature and throughout biology, geology, chemistry, physics, and astronomy.

SPIRITUAL PRACTICE

MANDALA

Praying with a mandala can be healing and a source of reflection of one's soul. Those of us who remain can lean into our wholeness and can find measures of solace and healing by reframing reconciliation as possible even beyond the bounds of death through work on our mandala.

- Begin with a breath prayer.

> **Inhale:** *Eternal center and circle of life*
> **Exhale:** *lead me in a love stronger than death.*

- Spend spiritual time with your loved one who has died by focusing on the four things that matter most: *Please forgive me. I forgive you. Thank you. I love you.* Designate each quadrant of your mandala with one of the four things, either in writing or by choosing a visual image. Then draw, color, write your conversation, or any combination of these.

- Now look at the entire mandala and ponder these questions. What quadrant captures your attention? What did you feel as you worked? What questions or insights arose as you worked? Place yourself in your work—where are you drawn? What colors do you notice?

- Write about your experience designing your mandala. Consider designing other mandalas for family members and friends.

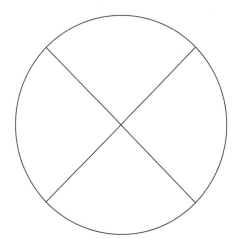

CHAPTER 9

HOW DO WE CARRY GRIEF FOREVER? LOVING IN SEPARATION

The reality of grief is far different from what others see from the outside.

There is pain in this world that you can't be cheered out of. You don't need solutions.

You don't need to move on from your grief. You need someone to see your grief,

To acknowledge it. You need someone to hold your hands while you stand there.

In blinking horror, staring at the hold that was your life. Some things cannot be fixed.

They can only be carried.

—Megan Devine

Conventional wisdom about healthy grief is that it will take us to a place where we are ready to "let go" or "find closure." Those of us who have experienced the death of loved ones find this language too simplistic, not helpful, and, put simply, false. Why on earth would we want to "let go" of those who have shaped our very being? How could we "close" that which has opened our hearts? Healthy grief is remembering and holding onto the goodness of those relationships. Healthy grief is opening our hearts so that the love inside can flow out into the world in great need of more love. Healthy grief is practicing different ways to carry the weight of our grief, which is love.

My mother died in the wee hours of the first Thursday of Lent 2008. That's the day after Ash Wednesday, when many Christians observe the beginning of the season of self-renunciation and examination leading up to Easter. The cross of ashes drawn on her forehead the day before remained.

I was not with her when she died, which produced an agony of regret I still feel. Instead of flying home on Ash Wednesday to be with her, I was administering the ashes on my beloved flock, in the congregation I served. Many religious traditions have a way of reminding us both of our own mortality and of the great cloud of witnesses that have gone before us. In the Ash Wednesday services, I repeated over and over again, "Remember that you are dust and to dust you shall return," as I imposed ashes on the foreheads of parishioners.

That day I was also making plans for a memorial service for a member who had died. I had planned to fly home that coming weekend to be with my mother, but now it was too late. How was I going to carry the weight of love and the reality that I had not been with her as she died?

Hours later, high in the clouds on the flight home, I thought about how my mom had given devotionals at the interdenominational Lenten luncheons in town. For years she had enjoyed putting energy, imagination, intelligence, and love into her preparation for these devotionals, until health and memory issues surfaced and part of the joy was replaced by anxiety. Now, seated thirty-five thousand feet above the earth, I could hear my mom say, in her irreverent and faith-filled humor, "I don't want to go on one more damn Lenten journey. Give me resurrection!"

Weeks after her death, I preached at a worship service. My sermon preparation had been filled with grief—tears, anger that life goes on, and sadness that life ends. The biblical passage was about Jesus as the Good Shepherd. My mom had had a soft spot for sheep and a sizable collection of them: paintings, ceramic and clay knick-knacks, coffee cups, pillows, scarves—you name it, she had a sheep on it. I had managed to write the sermon. Now I sat behind the pulpit, awaiting the beginning of the service. My breath-prayer mantra was, "Good Shepherd, I'm prepared; Guide me in preaching your word."

The prelude began. It was Isaac Watts's paraphrase of Psalm 23: "My Shepherd Will Supply My Need." We had sung that very hymn at my mother's memorial service, and I was not prepared to sing it now. I began crying and wiping my tears on the sleeve of my Geneva gown. Thankfully the tall pulpit gave me some privacy. When the hymn ended with the words, "No more a stranger, or a guest / But like a child at home," I got perilously close to sobbing.

Just then, as the congregation sat down, there came an oh-so-familiar voice. I heard my mom's warm but slightly exasperated voice: "Oh, for Christ's sake, get up and preach!"

So I took a deep breath, pushed myself up from the pew near the pulpit, and did just that.

Although I can no longer physically see my mom, I hear her loud and clear. These and other similar spiritual encounters with my mom comfort and assure me. I hear her faith, her tough encouragement, the things she taught me (especially when I'm at the bridge table), and her laughter. These occasions assure me that my mom's love is stronger than death and that I will forever carry this love.

I once shared these stories in a bereavement workshop. I was familiar with the metaphors of closure and letting go, but those didn't describe my experience. Processing my grief about my mother's death meant finding ways to keep her voice and presence with me rather than letting it go. After I had shared these stories, a professional counselor whose brother had died recently commented, "You've just reframed your grief."

He's right. Bereavement professionals have defined reframing in various ways. Thomas Attig, author of *How We Grieve: Relearning the World*, says reframing sits at the heart of grief, which requires a relearning of ways to love. He writes that the heart of grief, its most difficult challenge, is not 'letting go' of those who have died but instead "making the transition from loving in presence to loving them in their absence." Reframing our grief is a way of carrying our grief and of loving in separation.

No matter how well we loved when our loved one was present, we need to learn ways to love in separation by reframing our thoughts, memories, and experiences. Reframing isn't easy, by any stretch of the imagination. It can be as emotionally strenuous as physically framing or reframing a building. The satisfaction of both endeavors, however, is rewarding and lasting. Reframing takes our grief and scaffolds it into stories that we can comfortably carry throughout our lives. This reframing, or loving in separation, is a means of keeping us connected to our loved ones.

Our stories are gifts to our hearts. Thomas Attig writes that "we can return to the stories deliberately for specific purposes {to refresh our memory or understanding or to seek new understanding} or as events in our lives remind us of [our loved ones] and of their continuing importance to us . . . we realize the eternal value of those lives."

Three of my friends have reframed portions of their grief in creative and spiritual ways and have graciously agreed to let me share portions of their stories in this chapter. They have managed to somehow keep relationships with their loved ones vibrant and meaningful, even after death. Hopefully, in reading their stories of reframing, you will find a measure of peace and perhaps be inspired to reframe your own.

THE PROXY

Nancy LeCroy's husband of thirty-three years, Jan, died in October 2013. For her, the ability to reframe grief began with a little black cat. "An animal's eyes have the power to speak a great language," wrote Martin Buber; for Nancy, that language was one of comfort and hope.

Early in my grief, I was lost, numb. I found I could focus on what was right in front of me, but little else. By necessity, I lived in the moment. One evening, just days after the death of my husband, Jan, I was in the garage feeding two familiar feral black cats (a task that had been Jan's), when a third black cat appeared. I remember thinking another wild sibling had found our townhome. But then she made eye contact with me, a long gaze. A moment later, I could hear her steady purr and felt her rub my leg.

Almost at once, she felt like an opportunity—a creature I could relax with, who wouldn't expect me to talk, who wouldn't make demands, but who might quietly comfort me. And in a way I cannot describe, she began to embody Jan's spirit, my loss, and my desire to be close to a living being. Just that simply, she became important to me.

Although I didn't let her in the house right away, I began to look for her, hope she would be outside, and pet her when she appeared. I remember thinking I didn't want to be obligated. But then she was so easy to open the door to, soon exploring my too-quiet home, setting up housekeeping, keeping me company. Before long we were housemates, respectful of and calm with each other. She had found a home. I had found a friend.

I heard her backstory from my next-door neighbor, Mike. He had met her at a roadside park near Jackson, Mississippi. Hungry and dirty, she had been brave enough to crawl into his car. He, in turn, had been kind enough to feed and tend her and even bring her back to Texas.

When she moved into my garage to escape Mike's big, noisy dog, she was recovering from great loss, just as I was. Perhaps her own experiences had taught her that she needed recovery time; perhaps she was ready to be still and heal. I like to think so because that's what she taught me—to go slow, to take small steps, to appreciate the simple day-to-day moments that meant I was functioning, at least. I named her Eudora, Dora for short, to honor my favorite Mississippi writer, Eudora Welty.

Looking back at our life together, we did help each other. Great loss opens wounds that need time to heal, and we two were in the same traumatized place. I fed her and created the comfort, space, and care she needed. She kept me company in my lonely bedroom. She stayed close for hours at a time, sometimes purring in her sleep. She gave me someone to talk to—someone who did not judge my tears. I still think of her as Jan's proxy in the way she helped me through the most difficult months of my life.

Now, some years later when she too is gone, I have found another black cat at the Humane Society, as lively as Dora was quiet. Her name is Bella, and she reminds me of the ways my grief journey has changed. My trek continues to be challenging at times, but now I can focus my mind, wend my way through a long "to do" list, offer comfort to others, and even feel joy. I do believe Dora was a great gift, a surprise package I was able to accept that helped me heal at the very beginning.

THE SYMBOL

Creating memorials to our loved ones can be an important part of reframing grief. When we move from "letting go" to loving in separation, tangible symbols—ribbons, rocks, a bench, a tree—can be critical.

Each year before the winter holidays, the nonprofit Faith & Grief installs a memorial arch at a park in downtown Dallas. People whose loved ones have died can write their loved one's name on a ribbon and tie it to the arch as a symbol of remembrance. Todd Atkins is a pastor who preached at the multifaith opening worship service for the arch in the fall of 2021. Here is a portion from his sermon, in which Todd emphasizes the importance of signs and symbols.

I've heard people describe grief as a mountain, but if grief is a high mountain, then "there ain't no mountain high enough." I've heard grief described as a river, but if grief is a river flowing to a great ocean, that means it is always flowing away from me, since rivers don't flow backward. These metaphors characterize grief; however, I think they are limited. I have learned to view grief as rocks.

As a child, I used to always carry rocks in my pockets. I had my reasons. My rocks were my means of defense, my entertainment, and my companions. My rocks were my defense against our street's large Chow dog, whose daily duty was to chase the neighborhood children. I'd throw rocks at that Chow to protect us.

Before I tell you how my rocks were my companions, let me tell you how much my mother despised the way I carried rocks in my pockets. All the rocks had sharp and jagged edges, and they would eventually rip my pockets. My mother had a solution for everything—even the rips in my pockets—so she told me to go to the creek to get smooth rocks.

After rainfalls, a creek across the street would fill with the water and run off. My brother and I would entertain ourselves for hours by skipping rocks across that creek. We'd count the number of skips and brag about who could make the most skips, which was usually me.

The rocks of my grief also entertain me because they represent memories that bring a smile to my face. Holding a rock, I remember my uncle J, whose catchphrase was "What you know good?" Or I remember my uncle Sunny, who, when someone tried to make him do something he wasn't ready to do, would fire back with "You're carrying me too fast."

In high school physical science, we learned rocks are not formed smooth, but if they are placed under flowing water, they become smooth over time. The flowing water is nature's sandpaper, grinding away the sharp and jagged edges and making them smooth.

Grief does not start out smooth. It often begins with many rough and jagged edges that can rip pockets; but over time, your tears can help create a smooth surface. This realization allowed me to redefine my tears and see my grief through a new lens. I am not crying; rather, I am sanding my rocks. I am not depressed; rather, I am just sanding my rocks. It is not a sad day; it's a good sanding day.

Smooth rocks are more aerodynamic, which makes them good to throw at charging dogs, and they also skip better across puddles. Finally, my rocks are my companions. They are the people who are in a "much better place." We stand upon a foundation that is held up by rocks that were laid and smoothed over years and generations. It is impossible to carry every rock in your pocket, but if you carry them in your heart, there is always room for one more.

THE LETTER

When Thomas Merton was asked about his decision to enter one of the Catholic Church's strictest and most ascetic monastic orders, he had an interesting answer. David Chernikoff summarizes Merton's response this way: "He didn't become a Trappist monk so he would suffer more than other people, but he did so because he wanted to learn to suffer more effectively."

Elaine Gantz-Wright's son, Elliot Everett Wright, was twenty-six years old at the time of his death in August 2018. Through our friendship, I've sensed Elaine's desire in suffering is similar to Thomas Merton's: that is, if we are all going to suffer in life, as we all will, we may as well learn to suffer effectively.

Elaine, whose writing you encountered earlier in the book, frequently speaks at Faith & Grief gatherings, where she shares "A Letter from Elliott." She wrote this letter in her son's voice after his death, as if he were writing to her. The spiritual practice at the end of this chapter involves writing a letter to or from your loved one. "Grief clouds your mind's eye and scuttles your sense of possibility," Elaine reflects. "Nothing feels right. So many directions, but no place to go. It's visceral bewilderment—figurative and physical, together and apart, curious and terrifying. How could this have possibly happened?"

> Dear Mom,
>
> I don't know what to say, but I feel the need to write.
>
> I guess that's one of my signature conundrums, or should I say compulsions? Mainly, I wanted to say that I am fine. Things are good here, Mom. I'm good. So, stop. Stop worrying.
>
> I hate to see you in such a constant state of misery. I watch you, and I wish I could ease your pain. I don't think I was ever fully aware of all the love there was around me.

However, I do know how much you hated my motorcycle. That's why I stopped talking about it. At that moment, on that gorgeous Sunday afternoon, it was the only thing that mattered to me—my mania gone awry, I suspect. I know you tried to psychoanalyze me all the time, but my demons were not yours to conquer.

I did not mean for this to happen, but it did. I can't change it. I'm sorry.

And I know how much you struggle to make sense of my death and my life, too. To figure it all out somehow—investigate, question, probe and inquire, but it is a mystery without a solution. Best to leave the deed unexplored. What's done cannot be undone. (Even threw in a bit of the Bard for you. He sends his salutations, by the way—in iambic pentameter, of course.)

I see you desperately trying to piece together all the facts and events—tracking my digital breadcrumbs to crack my code, *but that will not help you.* Trust me. Remember when you tried to put parent controls on our first PC when I was fourteen, and I hacked it before you even noticed? Think about it. That's why it's been almost impossible for you to get anywhere or find anything.

I hate to see you cry so much and feel so guilty. There is absolutely nothing you could have done to change what happened. *Nothing.* I promise.

Remember when that spiritual medium person you saw told you there is a greater agenda you could not possibly comprehend? Well, though I was always pretty skeptical about all that woo-woo crap, she was right in this case. Totally dope. You would not believe it . . . but that's all I can say.

Unavoidable. Soul agreement. Above my paygrade.

It just sucks for everyone else. I don't know why, but I do know a few things: Life has not been easy for you, Mom. So much struggle, disappointment, pain, and loss. I know you tried so hard, and I never thanked you. I want you to be happy. And I know Ian and I have not been the easiest, either, but we are your greatest loves. Don't question if I knew how much you loved me. I knew. *I know.* Sorry I never did a decent job of telling you how I felt. I did not know how.

You were there all along, despite the rampant dysfunction of our family tree. You were there through the good, the mediocre—and the awful. Frankly, I think you took on more than your share. There is so much I never told you—and you will never know. Please be OK with that.

You are frustrated about so many things right now, but just a quick reminder—we are all on our own journeys. That sounds like a cliché, but it's the truth. In particular, be patient with Ian. He will find his way. He is carrying all the expectations of a generation on his shoulders. Let him find his own path in his own time. I know it's difficult sometimes. Life is so damn short, as I abruptly discovered. Oh, bad joke, but hey. It is what it is. (I know you hate that saying.)

No matter what, I'm here with you but maybe not in the way you expect. I know I seem aloof and hard to find, but that's how I always was, right? Look for me. That serene white egret you see on the creek when you walk. The bright cottony jet trails that dissect the cerulean sky on sundrenched days. The kind words and gestures from others who care about you. The surprising, esoteric stories on NPR about Japan, bitcoin, dead saxophonists, David Foster Wallace—though you feel abandoned by so many.

I hear you say goodnight each evening, and I see you cringe when you open your eyes each morning. I can tell that sometimes you feel like you can't go on. Please keep going. Live. Find joy. Don't let go of life.

Oh, and one caveat, the earth does seem to be in a radical reset right now—in more ways than you know. This virus stuff and the civil unrest . . . just the overture. *Maybe, my timing was not so bad after all, right?!* But seriously—you can't control it, any of it. Keep writing and take care of yourself. That's all you can do. I will always be part of you—for all eternity. Though I didn't say it out loud when you said it to me all the time, *I love you, Mom.*

—*Elliot*

P.S. Patches says meow. Give "Ace Landers" a hug for me.

CONNECTING ACROSS THE GAP

Many people have noted that, with text messages, tweets, and emails, writing letters is rapidly becoming a lost art. But writing a letter can help us extend and elaborate our thoughts and process our feelings. I have a few bundles of letters that Bob wrote to me during the days of our passionate courtship. How I wish there were more. Each year on my birthday, I pull them out and read them, because they are written records of our love affair. They are treasures. My sister, Alice, is a consummate letter writer. Reading her letters is like seeing her sit in front of me and hearing about her activities and her upcoming plans. They, too, are treasures.

While Bob and I were on the journey of Alzheimer's, former students and friends would write him letters. As I read the letters to him, a smile would cross his face with a hint that he remembered the friend and the times they wrote about. After reading the letters, I would place them on the table next to where he was sitting. Throughout the day, he would pick them up, turn them over, and hold them for extended periods of time. When I would sit by him throughout the day, I would reread the letters and he would respond like it was the first time he had heard the message. Like Bob and Alice's letters, memories of these letters, too, are treasures.

Reading letters from loved ones, both dead and living, can make them feel close to us. But have you ever considered writing a letter to a loved one who has died? Or *from* them? While it may sound strange at first—to write a letter to someone who can't receive it or to write a letter in the voice of someone who has died—people in grief report that it is a healing act of reframing. While we may not think of letter writing as a spiritual practice, it is deeply spiritual insofar as it connects us to another human spirit. Writing prayerfully, we connect with God and our loved one. Writing honestly, we stop trying to let go of our loved one. Writing across the gap between the living and the dead, we learn to see ourselves as loving them in separation.

SPIRITUAL PRACTICE

LETTER WRITING

This spiritual practice can be especially helpful if you have an unresolved conflict with or question for your loved one. Write the first letter to your loved one about the persistent feelings you have around this topic. Then write a second letter, a day or two later, from your loved one, responding to your letter.

- Find paper, a pen or pencil, and a comfortable place to write. You may want to light a candle and place it close by as a reminder that the Spirit of love is aflame. Decide if you want to write a letter to your loved one or from your loved one.

- Center your thoughts with the following breath prayer:

  Inhale: *Grace and peace within me.*
  Exhale: *Grace and peace around me.*

- Begin writing. Start with the day's date and a salutation, *Dear* (what you most often called your loved *or* what your loved one called you). Some writing prompts are below, if needed.

  ○ **From you to your loved one:**
  This morning I wanted to tell you . . .
  I'm thinking about doing something out of the ordinary and want to run it by you . . .
  Since your death I've been surprised by . . .

  ○ **From your loved one to you:**
  Out of the blue, I thought about when . . .
  I've got a new perspective and most of all I want you to . . .
  Have you heard me tell you lately, . . .

- After you have completed writing the letter, read it aloud.

- Reflect and record the thoughts and feelings you experienced in this letter writing practice. What surprised you the most about the experience? Did you feel closer or more distant from your loved one? What emotions surfaced? What would you do differently next time?

CHAPTER 10

WHERE DO YOU GO FROM HERE? DISCERNING THE FUTURE

I can make it for a day or two without you

And maybe I can make it through the night

I can laugh and I can drink and probably be alright until morning

But what am I gonna do with the rest of my life?

—Merle Haggard

What am I gonna do now? In any moment of transition, we ask ourselves—and others—versions of the question that Merle Haggard asks in his song. We've likely asked this question many times—after graduations, after job offers and retirements (does anyone retire just once anymore?), after completion of energizing projects, and when, after the death of a loved one, life is interrupted, stopped, and stalled.

After Bob died, the question marks in my mind simply multiplied. Am I going to sleep on his side of the bed now? Will I keep going for yogurt on Sunday afternoons? Am I going to use his favorite cup for morning coffee? Do I keep his comb, his sunglasses, his bottle of aftershave?

The questions popped up from my friends, too. Can you play bridge? What part of the day do you miss Bob the most? Can we go for a walk? Want to join us for dinner tonight? Can you preach for me, or aren't you ready to do that yet?

They popped up from strangers and acquaintances who knew he had died. Are you going to stay in your home? Are you going to move to another city? Where's your pal—I mean, didn't you used to always walk together around ten o'clock each morning?

The question—What was I going to do now?—left me with painful feelings that I'd rate somewhere between a 4 (Distressing) and a 5 (Very Distressing) on one of those pain charts in a doctor's office. The description for this pain: Interferes significantly with daily living activities. Requires lifestyle changes. Patient remains independent.

Another version of the question hurt even more: What was I going do with the *rest of my life*? On that one I vacillated between an 8 (Utterly Horrible) and a 9 (Excruciating Unbearable). Early in life, the question about what you're going to do with the rest of your life can prompt excitement about opportunities ahead as well as a bit of worry and fear. But later on, especially after a spouse dies, the questions about what comes next take a turn.

For me, those questions appeared like holograms in every room of our quiet, empty, and memory-filled home. For the first time in my sixty-plus years of life, I lived alone. For the first time in my life, I wasn't overwhelmed with responsibilities. For the first time in my life, I wasn't checking off a mental to-do list. Because there wasn't anything—not a single matter—that needed my attention.

After a loved one dies, the persistent questions about what we are going to *do* in the future can seem unbearable. But turning that question slightly might help us see the future in a different light. What if, instead of asking what we are going to *do* now, we ask: Who do I want to *be* now?

Exploring this question—of who we are becoming—leads us on spiritual paths of discernment. Like any transition season, bereavement is a time in which we need to discern next steps. So while thinking about the future is often the last thing we want to do in our grief, it is to questions of discernment that we now turn.

When I discerned, through years of grief, that I could do nothing to change the character of my daughters' father and that I did not want to change my own set of values, I chose to do the unthinkable: file for divorce. In divorce, the fireworks of new love turn into fireworks of grief and often vitriol. The grief involves a mini-death of grand hopes and dreams for a happily-ever-after life.

The grief work of divorce is in some ways similar to that of bereavement—full of anguish, fear, and regrets. When the time came for me to sign the final papers for divorce, I walked across the street to the courthouse during my lunch hour so that I wouldn't miss any work. I remember thinking how different walking across a street was from walking down the aisle.

When I returned, my boss met me at the office door and invited me to sit on the steps and share my thoughts and feelings. "I *think* I'm going to be OK," I said. "But I *feel* like I am in a deep, deep, dark hole."

"Stay in that hole," he told me. "Don't hurry and try to scramble out of it. Stay there until you decide who you want to be after you crawl out."

I politely thanked him for his advice—all the while thinking it was the most god-awful thing I'd ever heard. Stay in that hole?! Who in their right mind would counsel someone to do *that*?

Strangely enough, I eventually found freedom in that deep, deep, dark hole. I began to view this time and space as a rare opportunity to explore my talents, skills, and dreams. Instead of viewing my life as limited, I chose to view it as full of possibilities. In this newfound freedom, I chose to *listen* in times of prayer rather than pleading my case or bargaining with God. And in this time of mourning, I heard a divine call to seminary.

That call changed my life and my daughters' lives—a radical beacon of hope that occurred in the process of mourning. Remember the definition of mourning we looked at in chapter 2? Mourning means choosing to respond to grief and bereavement in life-affirming ways. When we mourn, it frees us up to discern well.

DISCERNMENT

What does it mean to discern the way forward? Before we define discernment, let's look at a story that shows what it is *not*. In *The Way of Discernment: Spiritual Practices for Decision Making*, Elizabeth Liebert writes about a young woman conversing with the director of a spiritual retreat. The young woman was talking about "her rising sense of generosity and her willingness to do God's will. 'I am just waiting,' she said, 'until Jesus tells me what he wants. When that happens, I will do it.' Her director, pausing a moment replied: 'Did it ever occur to you that maybe God is waiting for you to decide what you want to do and will join you there?'"

This story reminds us that we can't just sit around to discern. "Discern" is a verb before it's a noun. It is active. To discern is to put the thoughts simmering on your heart into a question, pose that question to the Divine, and listen for a holy invitation or clarification to your question.

The discernment process after the death of a loved one is distinct from the discernment we might do when we're choosing a job or a spouse or a place to live. Discernment involves the weighing of different values and goals and the prioritizing of some of the expense of others. After a loved one dies, we, the survivors, craft a new and abridged set of values. You know the list of "What *Really* Matters" that we all carry through life? We have shortened it. Drastically. Think about what you used to put on that list—and what you would put on it now.

Discernment is deeply spiritual, highly theological, and eminently practical. Basically, discernment is a fancy word for the process otherwise known as just trying to figure it all out. Discernment takes passion, faith, prayer, patience, and courage. Let's take a closer look at each of the ingredients that go into figuring it out.

PASSION

When grief seems to have stripped away every meaningful component of our lives, passion, like many other aspects of life, can appear to go missing. Passion perceives that we need time and space to grieve; therefore, out of love and kindness, it chooses to go into hibernation for a while. Passion, however, never truly leaves. As Nelson Mandela said, passion will not allow for "settling for a life that is less than the one you are capable of living."

Passion is our intrinsic motivator, our extrinsic determination of value, and the context for our prayers. Passion is our source of enthusiasm, which derives from the Greek word *entheos*: *en* (with) and *Theos* (God).

Saint Ignatius of Loyola believed that joy springs from our passion. Therefore, he crafted a daily prayer of examen as a means of recording daily joys (consolations) and frustrations (desolations). Doing the examen regularly can help us to identify or affirm our passion. The examen will serve as our spiritual practice for this chapter.

After his retirement and the death of his wife, Ralph discovered that volunteering at his church, a nearby school, and a children's home brought him joy. After the death of her husband, Ann learned that she found joy in helping women coordinate articles of clothing so that they felt beautiful. She started working in a boutique and enjoyed the extra money she earned. Nicci found meaning as she cared and advocated for her grandmother through cancer treatments. After her grandmother's death, Nicci changed her degree plan to become an oncology nurse. Each of them, while walking through grief, discovered a passion.

Dr. Perryn Rice, a Presbyterian pastor, offered in a sermon this helpful idea as a way of identifying our passion. He suggested, "Think about what makes you angry. Really angry." Children going to bed hungry, or food deserts? Families sleeping on streets? Lack of affordable housing? Deaths by suicide? Racial injustice? Decrease in the arts taught in schools or communities? Graffiti on public buildings? Rampant addiction? Health workers and public servants being underappreciated? Society ignoring people suffering from mental illness?

Isolation of the sick and elderly, along with their caregivers? Something else? Follow whatever makes you furious, Dr. Rice suggests, because it can lead you to your passion.

Jane became angry when her granddaughter with learning differences no longer had social opportunities and life skills classes after she reached puberty. Jane had the idea to start such a program for the community. It was designed for teens and adults with special needs and for their parents with needs for respite. The participants learned about their faith tradition, designed and led worship, planted a garden, cooked meals, and danced the night away at parties planned just for them.

Whether we try out a new volunteer opportunity or follow our anger or find our passion in some other way, figuring out our passion can help us discern next steps.

FAITH

Faith is a continuous gift from God available to all people. Whether or not we choose to accept the gift of faith and trust in its ultimate goodness has an immeasurable amount to do with what we believe about God.

For years, after church on Sunday, I'd make my way to the grocery store to discern (or figure out) what Bob and I would have for lunch. I'd toss a few items that looked easy to prepare into the basket and make my way to the checkout counter. One Sunday, a clerk looked at my clerical collar and said, "I don't believe in God." That made me smile. I placed my items in my reusable bag and said, "Well, I believe that God believes in *you*!"

And I still believe that. In some ways, whether we "believe in God" matters little. If God believes in *us*, sometimes that's just enough to make our grief bearable. Sharon, one of the cofounders of Faith & Grief, found that the gift of faith sustained her while her husband, Tom, received years of treatment for a glioblastoma. Her faith kept her going as she supported herself and their eleven-year-old son after Tom's death. Sharon's bereavement and mourning were bearable because she believed that she and her son were held in God's benevolent care. She was also thankful that the amount of faith she received from God, on any given day, was sufficient. Trusting that God believes in us helps us survive seasons of grief.

Faith opens our eyes to see and our ears to hear. The Hebrew Bible contains a story about Moses encountering the presence of God through a burning bush in the wilderness. One interpretation of that story is that the bush was *always* afire, yet never consumed, with God's love. Perhaps travelers walking by that bush each day simply didn't notice that it was aflame. Only Moses noticed it, and therefore only Moses had an encounter with God.

While you are in the process of discernment, pay attention. Notice. Open yourself to wonder. Ponder what God may be saying to you. One friend shared that each time he has been discerning a major transition in his life, he notices not one, not two, but three red-tail hawks perched or flying by him.

Notice. Open yourself to wonder. Ponder what God may be saying to you through serendipitous encounters. A relative became intrigued by the chance meetings with people and the pursuing conversations. He was astonished by learning there were connections between these people of which he was unaware. The information he gained from the six-degrees-of-separation conversations became stepping-stones in his discernment process.

Notice. Open yourself to wonder. Ponder what God may be saying to you through dreams that won't vanish at break of dawn. A middle-aged woman entrenched in corporate life could never turn herself loose from her deep desire to engage in ministry. After a corporate downsizing during COVID-19, she completed requirements via online classes to become a commissioned lay pastor. She now serves a congregation in pastoral care.

In the resource section, you will find a Jewish prayer, the Amidah, that may help you experience wonder and God's faith in you. When you find that you are having a hard time with faith, try asking yourself: What if God believes in me?

PRAYER

Mana Bailey spoke at a Faith & Grief gathering after John, her husband, died. We asked her to speak about ways her faith intersects with her grief. She captured the participants' attention right from the start by saying, "After John died, I quit praying." She paused dramatically and then added: "I just started talking to God."

A teenage boy, reflecting about his summer at church camp, once said to me, "When I'm here, it's easy to talk to God. Even better, when I'm here, it's easy to *listen* to God."

Prayer is conversation with the living God. A simple spiritual practice that can guide this conversation calls for time in a quiet setting, a piece of paper, and a writing instrument. Fold the paper in half vertically (longwise). It may help to write your name at the top of the left side, and the name for the Divine that you use on the top right side. On the left side, write a prayer of your deepest desire for your future. Read your prayer aloud and ask the Divine to hold that prayer for you. Quietly enjoy being in God's holy presence. Listen for words that enter your heart. Record emotions and thoughts that stir within you on the right side of the paper. Take a few moments to look around for an earthly connection to your desire. Depending on the time and paper available, continue this conversation with another desire, or the original desire written in new words. This process of discernment takes time, trust, and patience. It's a refining process. I remember the first time I practiced it, some ten years ago. I wrote, "What am I to do?" After listening, I started being more "specifically general." I wrote, "God, how can I use the gifts you have given me and have more time with my family?"

Another spiritual practice for times of discernment is similar. Rather than focusing on the desires for your future, though, engage in conversation with God about your past. Again, in a quiet setting, and with a piece of paper and writing instrument, allow God to sit beside you. Recall your desires when you were five years old. What did you want to be when you grew up? Write a prayer expressing that desire, and hear God engage with your inner child. Continue the practice recalling when you were eighteen, thirty, or another age. What did you long for? What would God say to you?

Notice ways your current and past desires are connected or disconnected. What feelings were awakened while having this conversation with God? How does our experience with prayer change when we acknowledge that prayer, like faith, is not self-initiated but a response to God's invitation to conversation?

By praying toward the future and recalling the past, we affirm God's ability to be everywhere at the same time, known as omnipresence. We may think of that word meaning that God is in all places, and that's true. But many religions share the idea that God was, is, and will be in all *times*—past, present, and future. Does focusing on God's presence across time change the way you grieve? The way you pray?

PATIENCE

One of life's biggest challenges for us is making friends with the mystery of time. After the death of a loved one, we, along with author Ingrid Betancourt, have learned "that the most precious gift someone can give us is time, because what gives time its value is death." We become keenly attuned to the fact that time is a precious gift and not to be wasted. This can result in us moving through our discernment process hastily, which may not lead us to the wisdom we seek.

When answers to the question "What am I going to do now?" don't readily present themselves, understanding the Daoist concept of *wu-wei* is helpful. Wu-wei is a humble and trust-filled approach to time. Wu-wei encourages us to relax, put our backs to the wind, and rest. It suggests that we not force a premature answer to a long-range question. Daoism contains a profound reverence for nature, and the serenity and patience we see in the natural world can instruct our souls.

Christians might say that wu-wei involves placing a higher trust in *kairos*, God's timing, than in *chronos*, secular time.

The Greeks had two words for time: *kairos*, meaning the right, critical, or opportune moment; and *chronos*, meaning the seconds, minutes, and hours that tick by each day.

Patience is the linchpin in the discernment process. It anchors us as we engage in the discernment process. I've never met anyone who states unequivocally, "Patience is my gift." The good news is that patience can be cultivated. We can practice it.

When I discerned a call to be a spiritual director, I wanted a certification as quickly as possible. The dean of a program for this field listened to me patiently as I balked at the three-year certification process. Didn't I get credit for years in pastoral care? Wasn't my doctor of ministry degree worth some advanced credit in the program? The dean listened to my every question, repeating the same answer: no. Before I left in a huff, the dean handed me an article to read about becoming a spiritual director.

I read the article and was humbled by a line it contained: "it takes a long time to make a pickle." Patience and peace entered my heart and it humbled me. I enrolled in a three-year program for spiritual direction. Time flew by. Each experience and each tincture of wisdom provided bread for my journey—opportunities presented themselves the following week to put into practice what I had learned.

Invite your soul to share its wisdom about your life—your God-given gifts, your skills, and your hidden desires. Invite your soul to remind you of the knowledge and encouragement you received from your loved one, and possibly the dreams your loved one always had for you.

This relaxed and focused time may nudge you to welcome a greater number of considerations to give meaning to your life. It may also allow you to hear the affirmation you long to hear from your loved one.

COURAGE

"What other people think of you is none of your business. It's their business." I've not forgotten this wisdom, spoken by a minister and counselor to a group of us in seminary. They're words I wish I had heard earlier in life—like way back in junior high. Remember this truth in the discernment process as well. It doesn't matter what anyone else thinks of your grief process. That's their business, not yours.

It takes courage to own our grief stories and to stop caring what other people think of them. Remember that list of "What *Really* Matters" that we talked about at the beginning of the chapter? The one that has gotten really short now that your loved one has died? Well, our lists may be shorter, and they may include different entries than they did before, yet each line item has now withstood grief's punch in the gut.

After someone dies, the loved one who remains often says, "I feel like I can do anything now, because nothing can hurt more than what I've gone through." This is courage talking. Our grief doesn't manufacture courage. Rather, it uncovers the courage already abiding within each of us.

In *The Book of Qualities*, J. Ruth Gendler wrote, "When Courage walks, it is clear that she has made the journey from loneliness to solitude. The people who told me she is stern were not lying; they just forgot to mention that she is kind." When this stern and kind attribute is stirred into the recipe for discernment, a newfound conviction and resilience set the course for us to go the distance.

Some unknown period of time usually transpires before courage makes the journey to solitude: the awareness of being alone without being lonely. It's equally important to never forget, not for one minute, that courage has walked you through this book.

You may recall that, in the first chapter, I congratulated you on the courage you have shown in beginning this journey through grief. I hope that now, with the confidence generated by self-compassion, you will be able to congratulate yourself, too.

HIDDEN JOYS

For years I have observed that certain people exude what I call "fullness of life" or "zest for living." Curious, I have tried to figure out why some people seem so alive and others seem numb or flat. Over time, I discovered a paradox: that is, those who radiate wisdom, joy, and compassion are often the very same people who have processed profound pain, tragedies, and injustices. They have lived through their own worst nightmares, and they are still standing. Joy and pain, writes Ann Voskamp, author of *One Thousand Gifts*, are "but two arteries of the one heart that pumps through all those who don't numb themselves to really living." Grief can make people bitter and numb, but when we choose to mourn rather than move on, we may discover, over time, a joy that we didn't know was possible.

Wisdom, spiritual maturity, and inner beauty come to us through grief. The Greek tragedian Aeschylus proclaimed repeatedly, "wisdom comes through suffering." Many times I have railed against this idea; other times I have experienced this very truth and observed it in others.

It's wise to refrain from speaking this truth to comfort others. Instead, any wisdom or joy that eventually comes through suffering usually arrives quietly, sneaking up on us when we're least expecting it. It's not a "lesson" we should expect or claim for others; instead, it's one we may discover for ourselves, over time.

Having taken some pottery classes, I sometimes imagine that grief is a potter. Grief has vision, patience, and love for its work in us. Grief sees fit to pinch out large amounts of clay to make a jar worthy to hold and carry the inextricably bound gifts of wisdom and joy. Without the work of a potter like grief, we are clay jars that lack the space or capacity for these gifts.

When a loved one dies, we may wonder whether we'll ever feel joy again. It can feel like happiness has hidden itself from us forever. Over time, however, we develop eyes to see the burning bushes around us—the presence of the sacred that permeates all things. By looking closely at the events and feelings we experience throughout a day, we may begin relocating our joy.

The prayer of examen, attributed to St. Ignatius of Loyola, provides a model for us to reflect, offer thanksgiving, seek forgiveness, and pray for ongoing awareness of the divine presence with us. This four-hundred-year-old prayer practice gives us a way to live more deeply and more mindfully in each day.

Our grief stories unfold in different ways. No one can tell our grief story for us, and no one can rush us along toward experiencing joy again. No one can tell us when this or that wave of grief will set us down. The story of our life unfolds as we cope with challenges and grief and seek stability in the midst of change. But within this story are glimpses of God's loving guidance, gifts of grace, companionship, and support along the way.

Tell your grief story. Carry your sorrow and befriend your emotions. Ride the waves and offer yourself compassion. Rely on your faith and your community and the spiritual practices in this book to help you. Learn not to "let go" or "move on" but to love in separation. Love still surrounds you. And love is stronger than death.

SPIRITUAL PRACTICE

THE EXAMEN

The examen is designed to be a daily prayer. Morning people usually like to review the previous day shortly after waking up; night owls may prefer to review the current day before bedtime. People who are organized especially enjoy this prayer because it has five clear steps; people who prefer less structure enjoy this prayer because it only has five steps. In any case, over time, the Spirit will open your eyes to patterns that will guide you and help you discern ways to increase joy in your life.

If you are interested in reading more about the examen, see Jim Manney, *A Simple, Life-Changing Prayer: Discovering the Power of St. Ignatius Loyola's Examen*, or Margaret Silf, *Inner Compass: An Invitation to Ignatian Spirituality*.

Here are the five steps of the prayer of examen.

1. **Ask God for light (illumination).** Determine to look at your day with God's eyes, not merely your own.
2. **Give thanks.** Gratitude is the hallmark of Ignatian spirituality. Ignatius wrote to a friend, "We will sooner tire of receiving [God's] gifts than [God will be] of giving them." Give thanks for life with God through the events of your day—the visible and invisible gifts.
3. **Review the day:** Think back over your day with God. Consider your interior moods, feelings, urges, reactions, emotions, or thought patterns associated with the day's experiences. Ignatius referred to these responses as spiritual "consolations" and "desolations." Consolations are things that increase our love for God, hope, charity toward others, sorrow for sin, interior joy, quiet, peace, movement toward God, a sense of hopeful purpose, and not being self-absorbed. Spiritual desolations are things like darkness of soul, unrest, focus on self, desire for base things, lack of confidence, faith, hope or love,

slothfulness, dryness, sadness, weight, separation from God, and thoughts that lead away from God.

Don't try to go over every minute of the day. Take your time at this point and rely on the Spirit's guidance as you remember.

> Possible prompts: *For what today are you most or least grateful?*
> *When did you feel closest to or most distant from God?*
> *What was your day's high point or low point?*
> *When did you feel yourself open to or block God's Spirit?*

4. **Face your shortcomings.** Ask God for forgiveness. Share with God specific ways you will show gratitude for God's forgiveness through your words, deeds, and the meditations of your heart.

5. **Look toward the day to come.** Where do you most need God in the coming day? Ask God to be with you tomorrow.

Take some time to reflect on or write about your experience with this prayer. What step was easy? Which was more difficult? What did you learn about yourself? About God?

RESOURCES

Religious traditions are replete with stories about death and prayers, songs, and rituals to help us navigate grief. Often, we listen to these stories and don't feel a visceral connection to them. Being in the process of grief ourselves can change that. We may discover the richness of spiritual wisdom in our own or another tradition.

The resources in this section come from a variety of religious traditions, and it's important to note that this is in no way an exhaustive collection. You may discover some aspects that may apply to your grief story or that will help you to ride the waves of your grief. Consider learning more about the religious tradition from which they emerge, and ask friends of faiths other than your own to help you understand their grief rituals better.

Rituals of grief and lament, whether experienced on our own or in community with others, can help us feel less alone. They connect us to other communities and individuals in grief, across both geography and time.

LITANY FOR RELEASE

This litany was written by Reverend Fran Pratt, a pastor, writer, musician, and mystic. Find more resources from The Reverend Pratt at www.franpratt.com.

God,
We humans have a tendency to hold onto things. Help me to loosen up and let go.

I release my fear to you, God.
I release my pain to you, God.
I release my uncertainty to you, God.
I release my shame to you, God.
I release my busyness and hurry to you, God.
I release my worry to you, God.
I release my defensiveness to you, God.

I release to you any feeling that I need to fake something, or put on a show.
I release to you any sense that I am unworthy, or unloved by you.
I release to you any interactions I've had with people that have hurt or shocked me.
I release to you any grudges or unforgiveness I'm holding.
I release to you any urge for vengeance or need to prove a point.

I release myself from inappropriate expectations put on me by other people.
I release myself from insisting on perfection.
I release myself from micromanaging situations, or taking too much responsibility.
I release myself from saying Yes when I should be saying No.
I release myself from saying No when I should be saying Yes.

I accept the peace you offer me in your presence.
I accept the rest you offer me in bearing my burdens.
I accept the freedom you offer me
  To not judge
  To not consume
  To not categorize or label
  To not fill silence with noise.
I accept the spaciousness that comes from giving up things that don't serve me or others.

Amen.

MOURNER'S KADDISH

Jewish mourners often recite the Kaddish during times of bereavement or on the anniversary of the death of a loved one. This prayer is spoken collectively.

Glorified and sanctified be God's great name throughout the world which He has created according to His will.

May He establish His kingdom in your lifetime and during your days, and within the life of the entire House of Israel, speedily and soon; and say, Amen.

May His great name be blessed forever and to all eternity.

Blessed and praised, glorified and exalted, extolled and honored, adored and lauded be the name of the Holy One, blessed be He, beyond all the blessings and hymns, praises and consolations that are ever spoken in the world; and say, Amen.

May there be abundant peace from heaven, and life, for us and for all Israel; and say, Amen.

He who creates peace in His celestial heights, may He create peace for us and for all Israel; and say, Amen.

THE PASCAL TRIDUUM

The first three readings below are usually read during the Paschal Triduum: the three days when Christians hear the story of Jesus that underscores life, death, and resurrection. Holy Saturday— the day between when Christians believe Jesus was crucified and resurrected—can be understood as a metaphor for grief. The disciples and friends of Jesus were overcome with grief, fear, sadness. The women attempted to do what was needed to stay busy. They were clueless about their future and what Jesus' death would mean. Many days after the death of our loved one are similar to Holy Saturday.

After you read the occurrences of each day, ponder the days surrounding your own loved one's death.

Friday: It was now about noon, and darkness came over the whole land until three in the afternoon, while the sun's light failed; and the curtain of the temple was torn in two. Then Jesus, crying with a loud voice, said, "Father, into your hands I comment my spirit." Having said this he breathed his last. (Luke 23:44–46)

- *What time did your loved one die?*
- *How long did the period of darkness descend on you?*
- *What role did your loved one play in this world?*
- *Who are additional people who experienced a "light failed" in their lives after your loved one's death?*
- *What were your words or thoughts after the death?*

Saturday: Now there was a good and righteous man named Joseph, who, though a member of the council, had not agreed to their plan and action. He came from the Jewish town of Arimathea, and he was waiting expectantly for the kingdom of God. This man went to Pilate and asked for the body of Jesus. Then he took it down, wrapped it in a linen cloth, and laid it in a rock-hewn tomb where no one had ever been laid. It was the day of preparation, and the Sabbath was beginning. The women who had come with him from Galilee followed, and they saw the tomb and how his body was laid. Then they returned and prepared spices and ointments. (Luke 23:50–56)

- *Who were people, like Joseph of Arimathea, who helped you after the death of your loved one?*
- *What day of the week did the death occur?*
- *Where did friends and family travel from to be with you?*
- *What preparations were needed?*
- *What, if any, fears or worries do you have since your loved one has died?*

Sunday: But on the first day of the week, at early dawn, they came to the tomb, taking the spices that they had prepared.

They found the stone rolled away from the tomb, but when they went in, they did not find the body. While they were perplexed about this, suddenly two men in dazzling clothes stood beside them, "Why do you look for the living among the dead? He is not here but has risen." (Luke 24:1–5)

- *With the imagination of your faith, how do you see your loved one resurrected?*
- *Where are the places that you most want to see your loved one?*
- *After Jesus's resurrection, he appeared before the disciples and said, "Peace." What would you want to hear your loved one say to you?*
- *Describe the moments of peace you shared with your loved one. What would peace look like for you now?*

THE AMIDAH

The Amidah is the core of every Jewish worship service. Some observant Jews recite it three times daily. Amidah means "standing"; therefore, the prayer is recited standing. This prayer encapsulates gratitude, faith, providence, and wonder. Stand and read the prayer aloud to hear God's devotion to you.

We thank You and sing Your praises—
for our lives that are in Your hands,
for our souls that are under Your care,
for Your miracles that accompany us each day,
and for Your wonders and Your gifts that are with us
each moment—evening, morning, and noon.

I WISH

This poem, written by Rabbi Shawn Zell, is for the occasion when one feels unable to grieve.

I wish I could bemoan the void in my life
Now that you are gone, *but I cannot.*
I can, however, help fill the lives of others
By putting a smile on their heart.

I wish I could cherish conversations
And visits with you, *but I cannot.*
I can, however, have meaningful conversations
That are cherished by others.

I wish I could recall sharing birthdays
And celebrations with you, *but I cannot.*
I can, however, make it a point to share
Birthdays and celebrations with family and friends.

I wish I could remember you
As my role model, *but I cannot.*
I can, however, strive to be a role model for others
And by doing so live on in them.

I wish I could express how much I will miss you,
but I cannot.
I can, however, share my love with others—
in the hope that my love remains with them.

I wish I could thank you for being a part of my life,
but I cannot.
I can, however, realize that you gave me life,
and for now, that has to be enough.

CHRISTIAN PRAYER FOR FORGIVENESS

Here is a prayer that Christians pray, with some variation, when seeking to forgive and be forgiven.

Our ongoing prayers in grief are filled with requests for our hearts to be filled with comfort and peace. Yet we fail to consider that forgiveness is the very foundation for peace.

God of grace and mercy, You know the contents or our hearts and still You love us. Guide us with Your steadfast love through the process of forgiveness. Shine Your light in the darkness of our anger, resentments, and pain. Grant us courage to examine our hearts and relationships. With holy tenderness, wipe away our tears to remind us that You are with us in this process. Direct our steps to cross the threshold of peace that passes all understanding and to enter into the joy of your salvation. Amen.

THE LABYRINTH

Prayer labyrinths, which are not mazes, date back more than four thousand years. "The labyrinth is an archetype, a divine imprint, found in all religious traditions in various forms around the world," writes Reverend Dr. Lauren Artress. "Walking the labyrinth is a spiritual discipline that invites us to trust the path, to surrender to the many turns our lives take, and to walk through the confusion, the fear, the anger, and grief that we cannot avoid experiencing as we live our earthly lives." You may be able to find a labyrinth near you that you can walk and pray. Or you can "walk" the labyrinth by tracing it with a finger of your nondominant hand. Slowly trace your finger along the path in the illustration, praying as you go. Set your own pace. The focus needs to remain on spending intentional time in meditation and not on questions of doing it "correctly" or when one step should begin or end.

Before you begin—Empty yourself of what keeps you from the Divine, and let go of a need to control your life. This releasing and emptying can help bring focus to a particular question or concern you wish to bring to the Divine, which then allows for opportunities of discernment.

At the center—Be fully present in the moment with the Divine and your loved one who has died. It is a time for engaging in conversation, giving time to listen. Some hear a literal word, some see visions, and others simply discover a newfound sense of peace and well-being. Some feel a shift in perspective or awareness, or discover a new insight; still others report no sense of change or greater awareness. This is not unlike any spiritual practice or prayer: some are powerful and moving while others leave us flat and uninspired, with many falling somewhere in between. What is significant here, as with all spiritual practices, is not the end result but the intentional seeking of being present with the Divine and your loved one.

Returning—Integrate any insight with gratitude by giving thanks for God being with you, both on the labyrinth and life's journey. Keep in mind that we do not enter the world or exit the labyrinth as the same person we were when we entered. A transformation has begun, whether we are aware of it or not.

ACKNOWLEDGMENTS

My immeasurable gratitude goes to Valerie Weaver-Zercher, acquisitions editor, for extending the invitation to write this book, for seeing a greater sum of the parts of potential and possibilities, for using her knack of moving paragraphs where they belong, and for encouraging me in the process. To Abby Perry, development editor, for her insights and suggestions, for her kindness melded with toughness that wouldn't let me settle. To Alice Duerksen, my sister and volunteer editor, for loving me, correcting me, laughing with me, and praying for me. To Sharon Balch, Wendy Fenn, Liz Harling, Shelley Craig, Susan Ingle, and Mike Shaw, Faith & Grief Ministries, hearts, souls, and minds for assisting and supporting me. To Tracy DePue, spiritual director, for reminding me that writing is a spiritual practice. To Amos Disasa and Meagan Findeis, pastors at First Presbyterian Church, Dallas, for giving me time and friendship. To Connie Webb, friend and Quote Sleuth, for sending me articles and listening while I untangled ideas. To Clay Brantley, Paul Burns, Brian Hardesty-Crouch, and Lil Smith, Wild Mustangs (pastors and spiritual directors), for the love, trust, and respect within our cohort. To Barbara Anderson, Wilma Honea, Cyndy Monie, Rita Odom, Barbara Pittenger, and Liz Williams for keeping the cards shuffled and ready to be dealt. To Margie Hackbarth Grossenbacher Allen, my aunt and advocate, for believing. To our children—Tammy and Rich; Diane and Jim; Omi and Robert; Sarah and Ken—

for loving and supporting me. To Natalie, Isabella, Kaya, Trey, and Stax, my grandchildren, for exuding hope. And to the robin-red breast for Bob-Bob-Bobbing in the backyard, by the patio door, and on walks with me.

This book is in memory of Barbara Grossenbacher Tilton and Naomi Powers Grossenbacher, my mom and grandmother, for their faith, strength, and love that is stronger than death.

This book is in honor of Jo and Michele for their perseverance, generosity, and delight in beauty.

NOTES

CHAPTER 1

attributed to Isak Dinesen: Quoted in Hannah Arendt, *The Human Condition*, 2nd ed. (Chicago: University of Chicago Press, 2018), 175.

Goraksha: For more on the Gorakṣaśataka, the early text from which this quotation originates, see James Mallinson, "The Original Gorakṣaśataka," in *Yoga in Practice*, ed. David Gordon White (Princeton, NJ: Princeton University Press, 2011), 257–72.

CHAPTER 2

loved one died: Asa K. Johansson and Agneta Grimby, "Anticipatory Grief among Close Relative of Patients in Hospice and Palliative Wards," *American Journal of Hospice and Palliative Medicine* 29, no. 2 (2012): 134–38.

"suicidal thoughts": Kimberly Shapiro, "Grief and Bereavement" (lecture, End of Life Symposium hosted by Compassionate Choices, December 17, 2021).

"body is killed": Ketika Garg, "In the Midst of Deep Grief, A Scholar Writes How Hindu Rituals Taught Her to Let Go," *The Conversation*, October 1, 2020, https://theconversation.com/in-the-midst-of-deep-grief-a-scholar -writes-how-hindu-rituals-taught-her-to-let-go-145370.

and buried: Elder Eugene Harry, "Preparing the Body for the Spir- it World," Canadian Virtual Hospice, accessed June 8, 2022, https:// livingmyculture.ca/culture/first-nations/preparing-the-body-for-the -spirit-world/.

"one's own way": Victor E. Frankl, *Man's Search for Meaning* (Boston: Beacon Press, 2006), 86.

the storyteller: Uri Hasson, quoted in Elena Renken, "How Stories Con- nect and Persuade Us," National Public Radio, April 11, 2020,

https://www.npr.org/sections/health-shots/2020/04/11/815573198
/how-stories-connect-and-persuade-us-unleashing-the-brain-power
-of-narrative.

"center down": Howard Thurman, *Meditations of The Heart* (Boston: Beacon Press, 1981), 28.

CHAPTER 3

"mental disorder": Ann Finkbeiner, "The Biology of Grief," *New York Times*, April 22, 2021, https://www.nytimes.com/2021/04/22/well/what -happens-in-the-body-during-grief.html.

immune system: For more on this research, see Mary-Frances O'Connor, *The Grieving Brain: The Surprising Science of How We Learn from Love and Loss* (New York: HarperOne, 2022).

"profoundly social urge": Robin Fox, "Food and Eating: An Anthropological Perspective," Social Issues Research Center, http://www.sirc.org /publik/foxfood.pdf.

"demographic group": "How Grief and Trauma Can Fuel Addictive Behaviors," Wellness Retreat, accessed June 8, 2022, https://wellnessretreat recovery.com/grief-and-trauma/.

"human experience": In his book *The Joy of Kindness*, Robert J. Furey attributes this quotation to Pierre Teilhard de Chardin (138). *You'll See It When You Believe It: The Way to Your Personal Transformation,* Wayne W. Dyer, Harper Collins, New York, 1989, epigraph of Chapter 2, "Thought." Quote attributed to Pierre Teilhard de Chardin, Wayne W. Dyer, Stephen R. Covey, George Gurdjeff, and anonymous. https://quote investigator.com/2019/06/20/spiritual/.

"isn't an explanation": Frederick Buechner, *Wishful Thinking: A Theological ABC* (San Francisco: Harper & Row, 1973), 46.

increasing size: Mary Hoff, "Shells Grow by Adding Chambers," Ask Nature, last updated August 18, 2016, https://asknature.org/strategy/shell -growth-through-compartmentalization/.

"center down:

CHAPTER 4

"meaningful pattern": Diane Ackerman, *A Natural History of the Senses* (New York: Vintage Books, e-book 1995), 2.

"years you have lived": Quoted in Diane Ackerman, *A Natural History,* 4.

"friend Mark Twain": Ackerman, *Natural History,* ebook, 2.

"day for growth": Virginia Satir, quoted in Christine Comaford, "Are You Getting Enough Hugs?" *Forbes,* August 22, 2020, https://www .forbes.com/sites/christinecomaford/2020/08/22/are-you-getting -enough-hugs/?sh=220943f768da.

"mourning is appropriate": "Study: Swedes Hug Anyone Except Their Boss," CBS News, November 29, 2007, https://www.cbsnews.com/news/study -swedes-hug-anyone-except-their-boss/.

"coming from": Ackerman, *Natural History,* 230.

"meaning is emotion": Kevin Berger, "Ingenious: Lisa Feldman Barrett," *Neuroscience,* March 30, 2017, https://nautil.us/ingenious-lisa -feldman-barrett-6010/.

"patient and kind": [Information about the research study.]

CHAPTER 5

"holding space for it": Naomi Oh, "A Posture of Surrender," *Clerestory Magazine,* accessed June 8, 2022, https://clerestorymag.com/essays/a -posture-of-surrender.

"turns it to gelatin": Joan Chittister, *Scarred by Struggle, Transformed by Hope* (Grand Rapids, MI: Eerdmans, 2003), 47.

"shared in the book": Walter Hooper, *C. S. Lewis: A Companion and Guide* (San Francisco: HarperCollins, 1996).

"I keep on swallowing": C. S. Lewis, *A Grief Observed* (New York: Harper-One, 2001), 1.

"tremble in perpetuity": Tim Lawrence, "Grief and Shame: An Unacceptable Combination," *Huffpost*, December 21, 2015, https://www.huffpost.com/entry/grief-and-shame-an-unacceptable-combination_b_8848712.

"been your delight": Khalil Gibran, "On Joy and Sorrow," in *The Prophet* (New York: Knopf, 1923), 12–13.

"warm and tender hand": Henri Nouwen, *The Road to Daybreak: A Spiritual Journey* (New York: Image, 1990), 157.

CHAPTER 6

starting with yourself: Jacqui Lewis, *Fierce Love: A Bold Path to Ferocious Courage and Rule-Breaking Kindness That Can Heal the World* (New York: Convergent, 2021), 19.

befriending our feelings: Kristin Neff, *Fierce Self-Compassion: How Women Can Harness Kindness to Speak Up, Claim Their Power and Thrive* (New York: HarperCollins, 2021), 3170.

"good about themselves": Neff, *Fierce Self-Compassion*, 3221.

coined these terms: Neff, *Fierce Self-Compassion*, 3240.

"ability to work for it": Neff, *Fierce Self-Compassion*, 3259.

"cost of commitment": Colin Murray Parks, *Bereavement: Studies of Grief in Adult Life*, 2nd ed. (New York: Routledge, 2009), 6.

nature is a form of self-compassion: Yasmina Abou-Hilal, "Self Compassion and Nature," University of Lincoln, https://studentlife.lincoln.ac.uk/2021/09/01/self-compassion-and-nature/.

CHAPTER 7

do their jobs well: Cathy Alter, "'Pandemic Grief' Proves Especially Devastating and Complex for Many in Mourning, Health Experts Say," *Washington Post*, March 28, 2021, https://www.washingtonpost.com/health /pandemic-grief-lasting-bereavement/2021/03/26/18ce5878-8be8 -11eb-9423-04079921c915_story.html.

"passage of time": Quoted in Alter, "Pandemic Grief."

"state of heightened alert": Julianne Holt-Lunstad, "The Double Pandemic of Social Isolation and COVID-19: Cross-Sector Policy Must Address Both," Health Affairs Forefront, June 22, 2020. https://www.healthaffairs .org/do/10.1377/forefront.20200609.53823/.

"profoundly freeing": Sobonfu Somé, "Embracing Grief: Surrendering to Your Sorrow Has the Power to Heal the Deepest of Wounds," http://www .sobonfu.com/articles/writings-by-sobonfu-2/embracing-grief/.

with 693 mass shootings: Jaclyn Diaz, "27 School Shootings Have Taken Place So Far This Year," National Public Radio, May 25, 2022, http:// www.npr.org/2022/05/24/1101050970/2022-school-shootings-so-far.

"cause pain for me": Albert Y. Hsu, *Grieving a Suicide: A Loved One's Search for Comfort, Answers, and Hope* (Downers Grove, IL: InterVarsity Press, 2017), 1148.

"uncertainty and anxiety": Karan Johnson, "The Surprising Power of Daily Rituals," BBC, September 14, 2021, https://www.bbc.com/future/article /20210914-how-rituals-help-us-to-deal-with-uncertainty-and-stress.

done with others: Henri J. M. Nouwen, *Out of Solitude: Three Meditations on the Christian Life* (Notre Dame, IN: Ave Maria Press, 2004), 195.

CHAPTER 8

"destroys family unity": Patricia Ennis, "Is Forgiveness Practiced in Your Home?" *Everyday Homemaker*, March 17, 2014, http://www

.everydayhomemaker.com/the-art-of-homemaking/2014/3/6/is -forgiveness-practiced-in-my-home/.

"say or didn't do": Litsa Williams, "Grief & Forgiveness Part One," *What's Your Grief* (blog), https://whatsyourgrief.com/grief-and-forgiveness/.

"we heal the world": Desmond M. Tutu and Mpho A. Tutu, *The Book of Forgiving: The Fourfold Path for Healing Ourselves and Our World*, ed. Douglas C. Abrams (New York: HarperOne), 76.

power of apology: "W.A.I.T.—Why Am I Talking?" TED★THE EMPOWERMENT DYNAMIC, May 26, 2017, originally run August 2015, https://powerofted.com/w-a-i-t-why-am-i-talking-1/.

Psychology Today *article:* Aaron Lazare, "Go Ahead, Say You're Sorry," *Psychology Today*, January 1995, last revised June 9, 2016, https://www .psychologytoday.com/us/articles/199501/go-ahead-say-youre-sorry.

"Thank you. I love you": Ira Byock, *The Four Things that Matter Most: A Book about Living* (New York: Atria Books), 46.

"divinity incarnate": C. G. Jung, *Memories, Dreams, Reflections*, trans. Richard and Clara Winston (New York: Vintage Books, 1989).

CHAPTER 9

"in their absence": Thomas Attig, *How We Grieve: Relearning the World*, rev. ed. (New York: Oxford University Press, 2011), xiii.

"value of those lives": Attig, *How We Grieve*, 179–80.

"suffer more effectively": David Chernikoff, "Poison into Medicine," *Spirituality & Health*, January / February 2022.

CHAPTER 10

"will join you there": Elizabeth Liebert, *The Way of Discernment: Spiritual Practices for Decision Making* (Louisville: Westminster John Knox Press, 2008), 30.

NOTES

"capable of living": Nelson Mandela, quoted by Henrik Edberg, "Nelson Mandela's Top 9 Fundamentals for Changing Your World," *Positivity Blog*, last updated April 15, 2021, https://www.positivityblog.com/nelson-mandelas-top-9-fundamentals-for-changing-your-world/.

your passion: Perryn Rice, sermon.

"value is death": Ingrid Betancourt, *Even Silence Has an End: My Six Years of Captivity in the Colombian Jungle*, trans. Alison Anderson (New York: Penguin Press, 2011), 143.

"she is kind": J. Ruth Gendler, *The Book of Qualities* (New York: Harper Perennial, 1988), 12.

"really living": Ann Voskamp, *One Thousand Gifts: A Dare to Live Fully Right Where You Are* (Grand Rapids: Zondervan, 2011), 84.

away from God: St. Ignatius of Loyola, *Spiritual Exercises of St. Ignatius* (Digireads.com Publishing, 2015), 316 and 317.

RESOURCES

"earthly lives": Lauren Artress, Creative Pilgrimage website, accessed June 8, 2022, https://www.creativepilgrimage.com/labyrinths.